MW00941396

Next Exit: Your Destiny

Next Exit: Your Destiny

Taking the road towards
the life of your dreams

Dr. Ebony Potts

ISBN:	Softcover	978-1-6641-4046-2
	eBook	978-1-6641-4045-5

Print information available on the last page.

Rev. date: 11/05/2020

To order additional copies of this book, contact:
Xlibris
844-714-8691
www.Xlibris.com
Orders@Xlibris.com
818390

Contents

Dedication

I have so many people that have helped me thus far on my journey. I would be remiss if I did not acknowledge my father, loving husband, in-laws, and beautiful children. You fill up and make my life whole; you are my reason. I don't take any of you for granted and love you with my whole heart.

I want to dedicate this book to four of the most influential women in my life: Carolyn Mathews and my three angels; Rommie Hill, Eva Mae Mitchell; and my mother, Sheilon Hill. You believed in me fiercely, spoke positivity over me, and taught me that any and everything is possible. You loved and guided me in a way that I can only hope to replicate with my own children. I thank God that I was fortunate enough to bask in your love, even if but for a short while.

Awakening—Definition

1: An act of wakening from sleep.

2: An act or moment of becoming suddenly aware of something.

Step 1

The Awakening—RISE UP!

Have you ever had a cold or a sinus infection? If you have, you know that for the most part, you can still function, but not optimally. You are up, out, and moving about your day, but not as your best self. When you have a cold, you go through the motions, but you do so as if you are moving through a fog. A dense fog that circles your mind, clouds your thoughts, and your senses. You feel like crap! You could sit on a pile of stinky gym clothes and you wouldn't be able to smell it. You can breathe, but not clearly. You can't taste your food. You use an endless number of tissues, as your nose becomes raw to the touch from blowing it. You just aren't firing on all cylinders. However, if you have a family, go to school, or have a job, you still are expected to perform. You are still expected to be whoever you are at work, school, or home. You oblige, but you do so as if you are dragging yourself through mud. You simply are not 100 percent. But one day, one glorious day, the angels sing, and the fog starts to lift! Your nose stops running like a toddler in a wide-open space, and the sinus pressure starts to subside. You can taste food again; you can smell clearly. The birds are chirping; the blue jays are singing. It is as if you have been awakened from a deep slumber!

One day, I was on the highway on my way to work, driving on Interstate 75, wading through Atlanta traffic. The traffic was so thick that we were only traveling about five miles per hour at times, on a six-lane highway. As a result, I could actually see my fellow commuters, those who were likely also on their way to work. I could see their facial expressions. Some individuals were frowning; some sat with their jaws clenched. As I continued to sit in traffic, I felt a familiar knot begin to creep into my stomach, and I started to feel stressed. I knew the route to the high school in which I worked perfectly. I knew that if I did not cross a particular mile marker by a specified time, I was going to be late, significantly late. Being late while holding the position I had at the school was problematic. Being even slightly late was an issue because I was often in charge of department meetings or my input and feedback was needed at board meetings. This meant it was unlikely that I could just slip into the school late and it go unnoticed. I would have a group of individuals awaiting my arrival. Eyes would focus on me judgingly as I entered the building. As I sat, contemplating just how late I would be, I thought about an article that I read, that correlated heart health with the amount of time spent commuting. The article stated that the more time an individual spent in traffic commuting daily, the more likely they were to have health issues that led to heart disease. Thinking about the stress that I was under at that moment, I completely understood!

As I crept along at a snail's pace, I looked to my left and then to my right and realized that almost everyone else looked stressed and unhappy as well. As I sat in the BMW I'd wanted since I was a child, a few miles from my three-thousand-square-foot Northwest Atlanta–area home, I realized that I was not excited about where I was at this point in my life. Although in my nearly twenty years in the field of education, I had worked with my share of ***interesting folks*** (wink, wink). My unhappiness at that point had nothing specific to do with the students that I'd worked with or any particular coworker, boss, or colleague. In all honesty (putting the few quack-jobs aside), I had also worked with some of the best at what they do, and the students were my absolute favorite part of my job. Any educator will tell you that! I just knew on the inside that I had reached a point where it was time to move on to the next chapter. However, when you looked at me from the outside, I looked like the embodiment of the American dream. I was the poster girl for all that they said you should have to be a happy, well-adjusted middle-aged adult. I had a McMansion, a luxury vehicle, a doctorate degree, a few bucks in the bank, and a husband that I referred to as ***man-pretty*** (wink, wink). However, something was still missing. As I continued to creep along in traffic, I thought to myself, I felt what my fellow commuters' faces expressed. I had acquired the fancy degrees that put a bunch of letters behind and a couple letters before my name. I had certainly racked up enough student loans to be someone important, even if I didn't hold as many strings as people thought I did. I had a loving husband and two kids. However, upon further self-examination, I realized that I didn't just feel this dis-ease that day. I often felt this way on my forty-five-minute commute to work. I was grateful, thankful, and knew that, by all measures, I was blessed; but I also knew that something was missing. I knew that I wanted more. I knew that I was not truly happy.

I was a part of the rat race. I felt like I was running on a hamster wheel daily. Chasing a metaphorical dangling piece of cheese. Cheese that I knew in my spirit I'd never get while on the wheel, and I hated it! The questions that now popped into my brain were, What am I going to do about it? How many other people felt this way? How had they, my fellow commuters, resolved to continue with what felt like an endless race? How did my rat race companions simply settle with this never-ending race as their reality, their final destination? Was I the only one that felt like I'd just had my blindfold removed and was then tossed into a sunny room? Am I just going to settle with being unhappy every single day? Is this what it means to be and adult, to be normal? I was told it was, but each time those words were uttered to me, something deep within me just wouldn't accept it. My gut just wouldn't align with the thought. I then remembered a quote that I saw by Ellen Goodman.

> ***Normal is getting dressed in clothes that you buy for work and driving through traffic in a car that you are still paying for—in order to get to the job you need to pay for the clothes and the car, and the house you leave vacant all day so you can afford to live in it.***

Insert loud, obnoxious sigh RIGHT HERE! I was this person. I woke up every day, shuffled our kids to and fro, paying a ridiculous amount for childcare just so I could arrive to work at the crack of dawn and stay until it was dark. I worked HARD and diligently, always trying to do my best. I watched as I was passed up for promotions based on politics, nepotism, cronyism, racism, sexism, and all the other *isms*. I worked ten- to twelve-hour shifts at times and sat in rush-hour traffic that often frazzled my nerves all the way home. On my way, I picked up our children and was often too tired to cook or be the mother and spouse I wanted to be for my family, arriving home as a big ray of sunshine—NOPE, not even close. My objective after work was to squeeze in just a few minutes of time to decompress from my long day in between dinner, my children's chatter, and trying to do for my husband. Once the children completed their homework, were bathed and fed, and my husband was tended to, I maybe had thirty minutes to an hour of time to relax, which often resulted in me falling asleep. Sleep—just to do it all over again in the morning (yay!). I would be up early the next day just to hop back on that treadmill, the hamster wheel, chasing that piece of cheese—cheese I'd never be able to reach from the wheel. I could see the cheese; I could smell the cheese. Some others had the cheese, at least I thought so. I wanted mine, but at this point, I realized I was just existing. Insert that obnoxiously loud sigh again RIGHT HERE!

Was this IT?! Was this how it was going to be for the duration? How depressing! If this was adultHOOD, this was the worst HOOD I'd ever been to. It kind of sucks here, if this was it. What a terrible existence. I didn't want to just exist; I wanted to LIVE. I didn't need to be Ricky Martin in his "Livin' La Vida Loca" video, but I definitely didn't want to be Eeyore, the Winnie the Pooh character, either! I wanted to live a life like I'd heard others describe and that I could only imagine. I just didn't know how.

One day I was watching TV, and I heard an old Oprah Winfrey interview in which she spoke about some of the things in her current, more abundant life that she appreciated. She stated that she appreciated not having to constantly worry about paying her bills and whether she could sustain her lifestyle long term in the back of her mind. She wasn't worried about sickness, job loss, etc., throwing her off course financially. She woke up every day feeling grateful for being able to do what she felt she was put on this earth to do. Oprah was in a profession that was in line with her vision for who she was as a person and what her God-given gifts were, and she enjoyed it. This was what I wanted too! Now I know that I'm no Oprah, but if Oprah can use her gifts to pull such a grand existence out of the universe that is in line with who she was as an individual, so could I.

I used this same mindset to help power me through some of my most difficult moments in college as a biology major and through obtaining my doctorate degree. When I struggled, when I wanted to give up, I told myself that the other students in my school were no better than I. If other minority students with humble beginnings could accomplish what they wanted for themselves and more, then so could I. I used this same tactic to attract the man of my dreams, my beloved soulmate. When I divorced my first husband, like many people who have gone through a divorce, I was very clear about what I wanted and what I didn't. Unlike my first go-round, I asked and prayed for a very specific mate. I refused to believe that God would draw some people to their soulmate and the love of their life, but that I would be left out in the cold, and I was right. The Lord did not love me any less than he loved others. God would not allow other people the privilege of accomplishing their goals and vision for their lives and then leave me on the sidelines, revoking this privilege from me. The universe was not out to slight little ol' me. How much wrong could I have done in my meager few years on this earth that the universe would work against me? I knew that was an insane conclusion. I didn't want my classmates' lives or Oprah's life. Well, maybe a little bit of Oprah's life wouldn't be so bad (tee-hee ☺). But what I really wanted to do was to live the best life God had for ME and my family. I wanted to go after my destiny!

In my quiet time, God often showed me flashes or glimpses of what my future would be. I'd always received what I'd come to believe were previews of great things to come for myself and my family. I received these visions in dreams and at times while I was awake. I knew the power in believing in these previews because, for the most part, all the visions for my life that God planted within me had come true. However, I knew that the next phase of visions would require bold steps and changes to my current mode of operating. I knew in my spirit that waking up every day doing what I knew wasn't a part of my next chapter, for an insufficient salary and marginal recognition for my efforts was not going to get me or my family there. Operating outside of the purpose that aligned with this next chapter for my life and from a place of unhappiness at the time was not going to get me the life I desired.

I took the next logical step in my career according to those around me and the degrees I had acquired, getting the promotion that many around me craved. I became a principal and spent hours working at a dizzying pace that left those around me in disbelief at how I managed it all. Yet something was still missing.

I knew many who were quite successful in their own right. I quizzed those whom I knew, about how to get what I was contemplating reaching for, but wasn't getting anywhere. The individuals that surrounded me were at my same level or were within what I'd call fingertip or tiptoe distance. If I wasn't where they were, the path to their existence was only a few yards away from where I stood. And to be honest, not one person I knew on a personal level had exactly what I desired. The vision the Lord had blessed me with was beyond my wildest dreams, one I had not witnessed close up.

I had simply existed for more years than I should have, but now over the course of a few years, I had been awakened from some slumber. That's the thing about reaching for the vision that God placed inside of you for your life. You often can't speak to, or get counsel from, those that existed with you on your previous level. You can't ask a worm about a giraffe-level view of the forest. If they knew how to get to the penthouse, why would they spend all their time on the floors below it? This is not to slight those with whom I sought counsel, but they simply did not offer advise that aligned with the vision that God had planted inside of me. How could they? Some had never seen the things that God showed me were in store for me. Additionally, the vision I saw was tailor-made for me. How could they completely or deeply understand it? At the time, I didn't have a blueprint to follow, an example, or a mentor to work with. What I did have was the desire for change, examples of how it was possible for others, faith, and a relentless spirit. I knew that I had done things before that were daunting and grew as a person. Each time I went through something scary, difficult, or trying, I learned from it. I was ready to step into the unknown. I wanted to lay claim to the life I wanted for myself and my family. I was AWAKE! I was done just doing and going through the motions. I wanted to LIVE life to the fullest, abundantly and within my God-given PURPOSE!

What about you? Are you awake? Have you woken up from your nap as well? Were your eyes wide shut? Do you finally realize that you are tired of helping the CEOs and/or executives at your place of employment live out their dreams, while you eat steak on payday and ramen noodles the next day and each day until payday rolls around again? Are you tired of not being able to afford to take your family on a nice vacation? Are you tired of living paycheck to paycheck or direct deposit to direct deposit? Are you ready for abundance? Are you ready to have your cup to runneth over so that you can help others? Do you want to spend more time doing what you love and with the people you love? Get out your pen and paper and follow the steps with fervor and diligence, because class is in session. Read, learn, and put into action the life you always envisioned for yourself. Take the next exit to your destiny!

The meaning of life is to find your gift;
the purpose of life is to give it away.

—Pablo Picasso

Step 2

Your Gift

In chapter 1, you completed step 1 on your path to your best life, the life that you dream of for yourself and your family. You are AWAKE! You have acknowledged that you want change. You have realized that you were not living the life you wanted for yourself and your family. You probably saw pieces of your existence mirrored in the mundane everyday life of what was once my life, which you read about in chapter 1. As you read along and saw the similarities, you knew you wanted a change too! A round of applause for you for taking the first step! In order to fix anything that is problematic, you must first realize that there is a problem. You have to see it in order to change it. You have to shake off the slumber of the regular and realize that it is perfectly alright to admit that you want more. What comes next, however, is often a little frightening. Next on your journey is a very reasonable question. Now what? Now that you have realized that there is a problem, now what? What is the next step? You know that you don't want the same as it has always been for you and perhaps all those around you. What do you do now? How do you break out of your current station in life? How do you leap from the ordinary into the extraordinary?

Moving from one station in life to the next often can seem overwhelming and unmanageable, especially when you don't initially have a mentor or a blueprint to follow. It can feel like trying to reach some mythical land of plenty without a map. However, we will approach this task in a step-by-step and easy-to-understand manner so that you can reach the life you have always yearned for! Breaking out of your current existence can seem as ridiculous as the thought of eating a whole elephant. Well, it's time to let out your inner fat girl/boy (I don't care how big you are—there is a bigger guy/girl inside that is always pushing you to have one more slice of cake—wink, wink J). However, even that task can be accomplished. How do you eat a whole elephant, you ask? Why, one bite at a time, of course! As Steve Harvey often says, "Inch by inch, everything's a cinch." And I'd rather be inching toward my own dream and vision for my life, the exit to my destiny, instead of using all my energy to power the dreams of my boss or some big corporation.

So what is the next step in this process? The next step involves you finding and identifying your own specific gifts and God-given talents. What is it that excites YOU? Don't think about money, cars, men, women, or fame. We are not trying to make you the star of a P. Diddy music video in the '90s. Don't think about what degrees you have or what path your parents think you should take. Don't think about what you have always done or what you have training in. Think about what it is that makes you feel good, fulfilled, or whole. What do you do effortlessly? What is something that you get compliments on? If you didn't have to work, take care of family, or worry about bills, what would you do with your time? What is your dream job? What is your passion? What is your gift?

Would you paint, work with children, or cook elaborate meals? Would you write, act, or organize events? What you need to figure out is, What's your gift? What are your special talents? What could you do for hours on end without feeling the humdrum, drudgery of "going to work"? What could you do on a daily basis that wouldn't have you sitting on the edge of your bed Sunday night, dreading Monday morning?

For some, it is easy to identify their gifts, but it is feasible that there are some individuals that have a hard time believing that they are gifted at anything. Many people, by the time they have reached thirty, forty, or fifty-plus years old, feel so beat down by previous wrong turns, missteps, and what they interpret as failed dreams that they allow self-doubt and previous circumstances to keep them from seeing exactly who they are. However, if you can read these words or comprehend them as they are read to you, you have a talent. We are all born with a gift!

> **Everyone has a purpose in life, a unique gift, or a special talent to give to others. And when we blend this unique talent with service to others, we experience the ecstasy and exultation of our own spirit, which is the ultimate goal of all goals. (Deepak Chopra)**

> **For we are God's handiwork, created in Christ Jesus to do good works, which God prepared in advance for us to do. (Ephesians 2:10)**

Some people know exactly what they are talented at. Some individuals know exactly where their gifts lie, and others do not. It is imperative that you take some time to figure out what your talents and/or gifts are. Why is knowing your gifts and talents so important, you ask? We will venture that, because you are reading this book, there are areas in your life that you believe could use some fine-tuning. You probably have yet to live your life to the fullest. If this is the case, knowing and acknowledging what you are talented at is the second step to living the life you envision for yourself and your family.

The power in knowing your unique set of talents and gifts will save you a lot of time, as well as perceived and real effort on your path to the life that you envision for yourself. The path from where you are today to the unique vision you have for your life will be full of pitfalls, roadblocks, and detours. It is not an easy road and will not happen overnight. If it was, everyone would be living their dream. No one would be on the road during rush hour, filing into neat rows of burned-out, unhappy workers, off to another day at a job that most of them hate. In chapter 1, when I was on the highway and finally realized that I was unhappy on my path, I would not have spent another four to five years trying to figure out how to navigate toward the vision in my head. However, don't be discouraged; don't let these facts make you veer off the path you just started on. Reading this book and following the steps outlined for you will help you to step toward your vision with a certainty not afforded to those fumbling around with no such guide. Knowing and using your gifts to their fullest potential can make your ride a thousand times more pleasant, palatable, and direct. Performing acts that lie within your God-given gifts often, in fact, bring pleasure within themselves. In fact, without using your talents as fuel for yourself as you travel the path to your ideal existence, you are less likely to reach your vision at all.

Most often, the Lord drops bread crumbs for us to follow—an idea, a vision, or a dream of you performing acts that lie within your gifts and or talents. You may dream of yourself owning a restaurant when in actuality you are a teacher. In your downtime, you may get an idea for a new invention that would make the lives of you and others you know easier. You might think of a way to improve on a product you use every day or think of a service that would be helpful for you and other consumers. We all have these little flashes of brilliance—breadcrumbs the Lord drops for us to follow that often would require us to use our God-given talents and gifts. Ideas that could very well power us toward the life of our dreams. Think about those little flashes, those moments of brilliance, the breadcrumbs. What talents would you need to have to see those ideas through? It is very likely that at you possess at least a portion of those talents and that the rest are obtainable.

Manifesting your vision will be one of the most challenging things you have ever done, but the payoff will also be better than even you can imagine. Finding your gift, the thing you can work hard at, get lost in, and sweat and grunt through without it feeling the sixty, eighty, or ninety hours a week it will take is key.

Can you imagine spending that much time at something you find mundane or even torturous for one, two, five, or ten years? Remember when you were in school? Remember your favorite and your least favorite class? In your worst class, remember staring at the clock for what felt like an hour while the teacher droned on until she/he sounded like Charlie Brown's teacher. Right about when you thought you couldn't take any more, and you were about to melt into a puddle of misery, you brought yourself to look at the clock and only ten minutes had passed? Now think about your favorite class, with your favorite teacher. It seemed like as soon as you sat down, class was over. Living out your best life, the best version of yourself, will take an enormous effort. If it didn't, everyone would be living the life. Using your gift will take the edge off the journey and can even make it pleasurable.

This is what the path to your ideal life, your vision, will be like, as powered by your unique God-given talents. If you love to draw, draw. If you love to sew, sew. Unhinge your thought process. Find your talents and gifts, nurture them, and take the shackles off your mind. When you find what you love and you grow your passion, the sky is the limit. Your path to your best life can be littered with the fruits of your labor of love. All you need to do is find your gift. Know that once you do, you are well on your way to your own land of milk and honey, figuratively and quite literally. Take some time to reflect on the questions at the beginning of this chapter, ask those who know you best, or take the talent assessment that follows this paragraph. Finding your talent and gift is one-half of step 2 and the key to your success on this path.

Career Interest Survey

In order to choose a career that will give you personal satisfaction, you must spend some time thinking about what really interests you. This activity helps you match your interests to different types of careers. For each item, circle the letter of the activity you would rather do. It doesn't matter if you like both of them a lot or dislike both of them a lot; just pick the one you would rather do, and circle that letter.

A – Operate a printing press B – Study the causes of earthquakes	E – Make three-dimensional items D – Analyze handwriting	L – Build kitchen cabinets N – Refinance a mortgage
C – Plant and harvest crops R – Replace a car window and fender	B – Design indoor sprinkler systems F – Run a factory sewing machine	A – Sing in a concert R – Direct the takeoff/landing of planes
E – Analyze reports and records F – Operate a machine	G – Develop personnel policies Q – Train racehorses	G – Operate a cash register B – Collect rocks
G – Work in an office H – Answer customer questions	D – Guard an office building H – Run a department store	G – Start a business L – Draft a blueprint
D – Write reports J – Help former prison inmates find work	A – Write for a newspaper G – Use a calculator	M – Assess student progress L – Design an airplane
L – Design a freeway M – Plan educational lessons	O – Help people at a mental health clinic L – Remodel old houses	O – Wrap a sprained ankle I – Guide an international tour group
N – Balance a checkbook O – Take an X-ray	M – Care for young children D – Locate a missing person	P – Solve technical problems J – Provide spiritual guidance to others
P – Write a computer program Q – Train animals	N – Plan estate disbursements/payments P – Enter data	Q – Manage a veterinary clinic K – Lead others
C – Be in charge of replanting forests A – Act in a TV show or movie	A – Design a book cover E – Build toys with written instructions	E – Operate heavy equipment Q – Manage a fish hatchery
D – Solve a burglary F – Check products for quality	B – Figure out why someone is sick R – Fly an airplane	F – Assemble cars K – Protect our borders
E – Build an airport G – Keep company business records	C – Learn how things grow and stay alive H – Sell cars	A – Play an instrument J – Plan activities for adult day care
F – Put together small tools P – Design a website	I – Work as a restaurant host or hostess D – Fight fires	C – Research soybean use in paint J – Provide consumer information
M – Tutor students Q – Work at a zoo	G – Keep payroll records for a company J – Work in a nursing home	D – Guard money in an armored car B – Study human behavior
J – Take care of children O – Plan special diets	G – Hire new staff O – Run ventilators/breathing machines	E – Fix a television set M – Run a school
A – Choreograph a dance K – Lobby or show support for a cause	R – Drive a taxi A – Broadcast the news	F – Fix a control panel J – Help friends with personal problems
H – Sell clothes E – Work with your hands	K – Audit taxes for the government B – Sort and date dinosaur bones	C – Oversee a logging crew B – Study weather conditions
I – Work at an amusement park N – Sell insurance	O – Give shots C – Design landscaping	R – Pack boxes at a warehouse A – Teach dancing
I – Learn about ethnic groups P – Manage an information system	P – Give tech support to computer users D – Work in a courtroom	O – Sterilize surgical instruments B – Study soil conditions
N – Appraise the value of a house M – File books at the library	Q – Care for injured animals I – Serve meals to customers	N – Play the stock market C – Protect the environment

M – Grade papers
R – Operate a train

L – Order building supplies
E – Paint motors

P – Develop new computer games
H – Buy merchandise for a store

K – Work to get someone elected
C – Identify plants in a forest

D – Guard inmates in a prison
L – Read blueprints

H – Line up concerts for a band
K – Ask people survey questions

E – Manage a factory
O – Work as a nurse in a hospital

A – Paint a portrait
K – Testify before Congress

B – Work with a microscope
I – Schedule tee times at a golf course

C – Classify plants
O – Transcribe medical records

F – Install rivets
Q – Raise worms

N – Balance accounts
M – Develop learning games

J – Read to sick people
P – Repair computers

F – Compare sizes and shapes of objects
Q – Fish

R – Repair bicycles
K – Deliver mail

M – Teach Special Education
P – Set up a tracking system

G – Manage a store
H – Advertise goods and services

R – Distribute supplies to dentists
I – Compete in a sports event

I – Check guests into a hotel
M – Teach adults to read

L – Follow step-by-step instructions
N – Collect past due bills

R – Inspect cargo containers
F – Work in a cannery

I – Coach a school sports team
P – Update a website

Q – Hunt
K – Enlist in a branch of the military

H – Sell sporting goods
J – Cut and style hair

B – Experiment to find new metals
N – Work in a bank

G – Work with computer programs
N – Loan money

L – Hang wallpaper
D – Make an arrest

O – Deliver babies
H – Persuade people to buy something

H – Stock shelves
I – Serve concession stand drinks

Career Evaluation

Count the number of times you circled each letter and record each number in the chart below.

A:	D:	G:	J:	M:	P:
B:	E:	H:	K:	N:	Q:
C:	F:	I:	L:	O:	R:

Now that you have the results from your career interest assessment, it's time to learn about specific career fields that match your interests.

Write down the two letters with the most responses. These are your top two areas of career interest. If you have a tie, list three:

_____ _____ _____

Find and read the description of your top area of career interest on the next page. Then, record your interest area(s) here:

____

____

____

Career Interest Areas

A. **Arts, A/V Technology and Communications:** Interest in creative or performing arts, communication or A/V technology.

B. **Science, Technology, Engineering and Mathematics:** Interest in problem-solving, discovering, collecting and analyzing information and applying findings to problems in science, math and engineering.

C. **Plants, Agriculture and Natural Resources:** Interest in activities involving plants, usually in an outdoor setting.

D. **Law, Public Safety, Corrections and Security:** Interest in judicial, legal and protective services for people and property.

E. **Mechanical Manufacturing:** Interest in applying mechanical principles to practical situations using machines, hand tools or techniques.

F. **Industrial Manufacturing:** Interest in repetitive, organized activities in a factory or industrial setting.

G. **Business, Management and Administration:** Interest in organizing, directing and evaluating business functions.

H. **Marketing, Sales and Service:** Interest in bringing others to a point of view through personal persuasion, using sales or promotional techniques.

I. **Hospitality and Tourism:** Interest in providing services to others in travel planning and hospitality services in hotels, restaurants and recreation.

J. **Human Services:** Interest in helping others with their mental, spiritual, social, physical or career needs.

K. **Government and Public Administration:** Interest in performing government functions at the local, state or federal level.

L. **Architecture, Design and Construction:** Interest in designing, planning, managing, building and maintaining physical structures.

M. **Education and Training:** Interest in planning, managing and providing educational services, including support services, library and information services.

N. **Finance, Banking, Investments and Insurance:** Interest in financial and investment planning and management, and providing banking and insurance services.

O. **Health Sciences, Care and Prevention:** Interest in helping others by providing diagnostic, therapeutic, informational and environmental services, including researching and developing new health care services.

P. **Information Technology (IT):** Interest in the design, development, support and management of hardware, software, multimedia, systems integration services and technical support.

Q. **Animals, Agriculture and Natural Resources:** Interest in activities involving the training, raising, feeding and caring for animals.

R. **Transportation, Distribution and Logistics:** Interest in the movement of people, materials and goods by road, pipeline, air, railroad or water.

Career Evaluation

Now that you know what career areas may interest you, explore some of the careers that fall in those categories below. Do you see any occupations you want to know more about? If so, those are the careers you might want to research as future occupations.

Agriculture, Animals and Natural Resources
- Agricultural Engineer
- Agricultural Scientist
- Animal Trainer
- Chef
- Conservation Scientist
- Farm Equipment Mechanic
- Fish and Game Warden
- Forester
- Veterinarian
- Zoologist

Architecture and Construction
- Architect
- Cabinetmaker
- Carpenter
- Construction Manager
- Electrician
- Civil Engineer
- General Construction Worker
- Highway Maintenance Worker
- Interior Designer
- Sheet Metal Worker
- Surveying and Mapping Technician

Arts, A/V Technology and Communications
- Actor
- Art Director
- Broadcast Technician
- Camera Operator
- Composer and Music Arranger
- Film and Video Editor
- Cartographer
- News Reporter
- Photographer
- Producer and Director
- Set and Exhibit Designer
- Technical Writer
- Graphic Designer

Business, Management and Administration
- Accountant
- Advertising Manager
- Computer Operator
- Court Reporter
- Management Analyst
- Meeting and Convention Planner
- Payroll Clerk
- Property and Real Estate Manager
- Shipping and Receiving Clerk
- Statistician

Education and Training
- Audio/Visual Specialist
- Coach and Sports Instructor
- College/University Administrator
- Teacher/Professor
- Librarian
- Public Health Educator
- Special Education Teacher
- Speech Pathologist

Finance
- Accounting Clerk
- Appraiser
- Credit Analyst
- Credit Checker
- Economist
- Financial Counselor
- Insurance Adjuster and Examiner
- Insurance Agent
- Loan Officer
- Tax Preparer

Government and Public Administration
- City Planning Aide
- Construction/Building Inspector
- Interpreter and Translator
- License Clerk
- Occupational Health Specialist
- Tax Examiner

Health Sciences
- Anesthesiologist
- Athletic Trainer
- Chiropractor
- Dentist
- Emergency Medical Technician
- Physical Therapist
- Occupational Therapist
- Pharmacist
- Physician
- Registered Nurse

Hospitality and Tourism
- Baggage Porter and Bellhop
- Chef and Dinner Cook
- Food Service Worker
- Hotel Manager
- Janitor/Housekeeper Supervisor
- Reservation and Ticket Agent
- Restaurant Manager
- Tour Guide
- Travel Agent

Human Services
- Child Care Worker
- Clergy
- Cosmetologist
- Counselor
- Funeral Director
- Manicurist
- Professional Makeup Artist
- Financial Adviser
- Psychologist
- Residential Counselor
- Social Worker

Information Technology (IT)
- Computer/Information Systems Manager
- Computer Engineer
- Computer Programmer
- Computer Security Specialist
- Computer Support Specialist
- Computer Systems Analyst
- Data Communications Analyst
- IT Mechanic

Law, Public Safety, Corrections and Security
- Coroner
- Corrections Officer
- Court Clerk
- Detective and Investigator
- Firefighter
- Judge
- Lawyer
- Life Guard and Ski Patrolman
- Police Patrol Officer

Manufacturing (Mechanical/Industrial)
- Chemical Engineer
- Forklift Operator
- Gas and Oil Plant Operator
- Jeweler
- Locksmith
- Metal/Plastic Processing Worker
- Office Machine Repairer
- Power Plant Operator
- Shoe and Leather Worker
- Welder

Marketing, Sales and Services
- Advertising Salesperson
- Buyer and Purchasing Agent
- Customer Service Representative
- Floral Designer
- Market Research Analyst
- Public Relations Specialist
- Real Estate Agent
- Sales Manager
- Telemarketer

Science, Technology, Engineering and Mathematics
- Aerospace Engineer
- Biologist
- Chemist
- Electrical and Electronics Engineer
- Geographer
- Petroleum Engineer
- Mechanical Engineer
- Meteorologist
- Physicist
- Safety Engineer

Transportation, Distribution and Logistics
- Air Traffic Controller
- Airplane Pilot
- Automobile Mechanic
- Flight Attendant
- Motorboat Mechanic
- School Bus Driver
- Subway and Streetcar Operator
- Traffic Technician
- Transportation Agent

Great! You have discovered your talent/gift, or at least you are on the path to doing so. So what should you do now, you ask? Many of you in this process may have found that you are gifted at multiple things, if you didn't know that already. Perhaps you have spent the last few years or even the last few decades operating in one area in which you are gifted, but you know that your time in that lane has run its course. Maybe you now realize that this particular talent does not align to your vision or your new path. Well, that is simple. TURN THE PAGE! Use one or a set of your other talents to work toward your ideal life. God is not stingy when he disperses talents and gifts to us. As you explore and discover your talents, the second half of step 2 on your path, is to learn, absorb, and take in as much information about your gifts as possible; then rinse, wash, and repeat! If you plan to use your gift as an income source, you need to learn as much as possible about your gift(s). You may be a talented hairstylist, but there are always new products and styles that your potential customers may be interested in. You may be great with children and be thinking about finally opening up your own daycare. What do you know about how a long-standing and successful daycare in your area has been able to sustain their business? Maybe you want to be a motivational speaker. Have you attended a training or session run by a successful motivational speaker that has visited your area? The key here is to learn and absorb information that you can use to start out on your path.

Although your parents, friends, and coworkers may be a good source of advice for many aspects of your life, they may not be great sources of info as you embark on this particular journey. You need to align yourself with people and information related to your gift and how to use it to power your vision. If you are trying to learn how to fly, you wouldn't ask a bus driver for advice, would you? If you want to be the next Serena Williams, you are not going read about and try to follow the trajectory of Magic Johnson, would you? These are the same reasons you WILL DEFINITELY have to look outside of your immediate circle, your comfort zone, to learn how to make your dreams a reality. Find at least two to three individuals that are currently successful at what you are reaching for and follow them, read their books, and learn as much as you can from them. Want to be a dentist? Find two to three local dentists near you that are willing to mentor you. Want to design a clothing line? Follow your favorite designers on social media, attend fashion shows, and locate your nearest fashion institute. Learn as much as possible. The objective once you figure out your talents and/or gifts is to be a sponge. Soak up as much information as you can. Learn how others have parlayed their passions into sustainable businesses so that you can follow in their footsteps. Follow those footsteps right into the life of your dreams.

Where there is no vision, the people perish.
—Proverbs 29:18 KJV

If you can imagine it, you can achieve it.
If you can dream it, you can become it
—William Author Ward

If you can see it in your mind, you
can hold it in your hand.
—Bob Proctor

If you dream it, you can do it.
—Walt Disney

So many of our dreams at first seem
impossible, then they seem improbable,
and then, when we summon the will,
they soon become inevitable.
—Christopher Reeve

A dream written down with a date
becomes a goal, a goal broken down into
steps becomes a plan, a plan backed by
action makes your dreams come true.
—Greg S. Reid

Visualizing is daydreaming with a purpose.
—Bo Bennett

What you imagine yourself to be,
you will become. When you visualize
something, your brain goes to work full
time to achieve what it has seen.
—Allison Grenier

Step 3

The Vision—What Life Do YOU Desire?

In your mind's eye, picture you living the life that you have always dreamed of for yourself. What if I told you that you could use the gifts or talents that you identified in chapter 2 to make your dream or vision come to fruition? What would that dream look like? This is not the time to be modest or play coy. Dream big!

In your wildest of wild dreams, what would you possess and who would you be? Pause and visualize it. Where are you? What are you doing, and where do you live? Who is with you, and what part do they play in your personal vision for your ideal existence? What kind of house would you have? What kind of car would you drive? Examine every important aspect of your life—what would they be like? If you could paint your health and your family, social, spiritual, and financial life into a perfect picture, what would it look like? Think, imagine, and visualize it! Close your eyes and meditate on this ideal existence for yourself. No—for real, close your eyes and imagine it. This is a very important step. Just don't go to sleep while you mediate on it; we have more to talk about! (Wink, wink.)

If you are a parent, I know that you probably fell asleep while meditating above. Totally understandable! But now that you are back, let's get back to dream-building. At some other time, before you purchased this book, you may have found yourself daydreaming about what kind of life you wished you had. The type of life you would create for yourself if only you won the Mega Million Powerball or any other big lottery drawing. How you would quit your job and tell your boss what you really think of them! (Insert all the expletives here.) Ooooooh, I'm telling your pastor (wink, wink). Who you would help (that's better!). Where you would travel, and what you would purchase. Which old boyfriend/girlfriend you would make regret the day they did you wrong (mmmm-hmmm). Who you would spend your time with, and what you would do with your time, if you had more time to use at your will. It is always fun to imagine your ideal existence; however, it sadly all comes crumbling down the moment you realize you didn't win. You check your numbers and see that you are not an instant millionaire, and now you relegate yourself to return to your ordinary existence (probably more expletives here—I won't tell this time). You pull out clothes for your next day at the job you can't stand, and sit on the edge of your bed on Sunday night disappointed, wishing for a different outcome Monday morning. We've all been there.

However, this is certainly not a recipe for success at living out your vision. Or perhaps your vision does not have that much to do with wild riches at all. Maybe you are at the point in life where you just want to find that special someone to spend your life with and create a family. Maybe your wildest dream is to be able to help as many people as you can who suffer from addiction, abuse, or other ailments that people often deal with in silence. Perhaps your vision encompasses bits and pieces of many things. Whatever your dream is, riding the highs and lows of hinging your dreams on the lotto, other people, or any other matter that is out of your control is the fastest and easiest way to live defeated and unfulfilled. You can't hinge your dreams on anyone or anything but yourself and the Creator, or you will never reach the potential that lies within you.

Living out your vision starts with you practicing the exercise that you did at the beginning of this chapter. Imagine it! Your imagination is your destination. The life you envision will become the goal; it is what you are striving for—your target! You can't ever get to your destination if you never establish where you are going.

Imagine that you are told that you could go on a cruise around the world for free. At first you may be extremely excited. Almost everyone that receives such news would surely and gladly embark on such a rare and unique opportunity. However, as you start to learn more and more about the upcoming journey, you are told that it has no definite end date. As you ponder this new information, you are also given the most poignant bit of news about your itinerary: the boat has no ultimate destination. There isn't a definite itinerary, no ports of call. The boat has no specific stops to ponder, plan for, or look forward to. You may get to see China and the Great Wall, or you might not. You may get to Morocco or get to see the Fiji Islands. You might not. You may journey to the Land Down Under, or you may not venture anywhere near Australia. Lastly, when the adventure is all said and done, where will you end up? How can you plan to disembark from the ship and return home if you have no idea where you are going and when you will get there? Who would embark on such a journey? Who would sign up to take part in what could be a journey filled with roadblocks, setups, and setbacks. A journey that not only has no end date but, most importantly, has NO DESTINATION IN MIND! I doubt that once you have ALL the information that you or anyone else in their right mind would go on such a journey. Any ship that does not have a destination will travel the water, aimlessly ending up in one area after the next, mishap after mishap, until it runs out of fuel. Our lives are the same way. Every day that you live without a vision or a goal in mind, you are on a journey to nowhere, very much like the imaginary journey described above. Most would agree that signing up for such a journey would be crazy, but many of us are on a very similar journey daily and aren't even aware of it! Are you bouncing from one thing to the next, one job to another, one relationship to the next aimlessly, knowing that one day you will run out of gas? What are you working toward? What kind of goals do you want to achieve? Are you actively trying to figure out what your goals are and strategically working toward them? What are you doing to make sure that you don't end up an old man or woman full of regrets? Full of thoughts about what you would have, should have, or could have done with your life? Do you want ordinary or extraordinary? It all starts with your vision.

Once you establish your vision and make honoring and going after that vision your goal, now when you get up in the morning, you have a goal. You are working toward something. You are no longer an aimless ship wandering through the sea of your life until you run out of gas. Your vision gives you purpose.

While constructing the visual representation of your ideal life in your mind's eye, leave no stone unturned. Your life has many facets that affect it. Your health, family, finances, spirituality, and social circle all affect your quality of life. Once you take the time to come up with a detailed and solid idea of what your vision is, write it down and be specific. A dream or vision written down now becomes a target, a goal. According to Dr. Gail Matthews, a psychology professor at the Dominican University in California, individuals that write down clear and detailed goals are 42 percent more likely to achieve them. Want to make your vision even more likely to come true? Make a visual. Make a vision board, add details like dates and steps for achievement, and meditate on it. Hang your visual somewhere you have to pass by it every day but is still private to you. Your vision board is to be a reminder to YOU, not a discussion piece for everyone that comes into your house. Read your written or visual display often. Say your dreams out loud to yourself often. Hearing your dream in your own voice is powerful; it also recenters you, realigns you. It's a silent tugging on your heart and mind that asks you daily, What are you doing to make this real? Constantly pulling on your conscious and subconscious mind to figure out how to get there. What connections do you have to make? Who do you know that can point you in the right direction? Write your goals on your bathroom mirror. Reflect daily on your goals as you get ready for bed and as you venture out into the world each morning. What could you have done during that specific day to inch you closer to the vision you have constructed in your head. What can you do tomorrow to make what you have placed on your vision board closer to becoming true? Put the law of attraction into use!

What is the law of attraction, you ask? The basic tenant of the law of attraction is that anything you focus on, speak about, and direct your energy toward puts magnetic energy out into the universe that draws the object you envision toward you. Every thought you have has a frequency, a vibration. The law of attraction states that your thoughts match the frequency of the object they center on. The energy released by your thoughts is believed to be magnetic. It attracts what it is centered on. The more you focus on a goal, you begin to attract that thing or those things to you. The more you think about and visualize a goal or vision, the more magnetic energy is being released to pull that object to you. The object(s) begin(s) to seek you and is drawn to you as much as you are drawn to it or them. Now to some, this may sound like a bunch of hocus-pocus insanity, but I assure you, it isn't. There are plenty of books besides this one, research, and even biblical backing for this concept. Don't believe it? Why do you think a baseball/softball coach tells you to swing through the ball when you hit it? Why would visualizing yourself swinging through a ball before you actually make contact with it help you? What about when that same coach tells you to keep your eyes on the baseball? He or she tells you this because whatever you focus on, your body has no choice but to follow through with and aim all its energy toward it! Why would writing your goals down improve the likelihood of them being accomplished? Why is a pole vaulter told to visualize themselves going over the pole BEFORE attempting to do so? For the same reason as described above: the law of attraction! The mind is a very powerful object. The more you reflect upon, think about, plan around, research, and visualize your vision, the more likely you are to manifest that goal or vision and bring it into existence. You have superpowers! Well, kind of (wink, wink). Through faith, Matthew 27:2 says that you can look at a mountain and cause it to move! Now don't go staring at mountains trying to move them around with your mind. If you manage to do that, look me up if you need a booking agent! The Bible is not talking about your ability to literally move landmasses. What is meant by this verse is that you can move the mountains, molehills, and potholes in your life and the lives of those around you. Faith is the visualization and belief in things that have yet to occur—another form of the law of attraction. Proverbs 23:7 states that, as a man thinks, so is he. Yet another example. There are thousands upon thousands more examples, quotes, books, etc., all that speak of the power of the law of attraction. By completing visualization exercises and the other practices suggested thus far, you are already beginning to harness the power of the law of attraction and put it to use to bring your vision to life.

Upon completion of your vision board and understanding its importance, you are three steps closer to achieving your dreams than you were before you picked up this book!

You have awakened to the fact that you want change and that you want something better, and that better is possible! Yes! You discovered that you don't want the ordinary and that you want to go after all you are destined for. You are done sitting on the sidelines of your life! Step 1, the awakening, is complete. Insert virtual high five here (***smack!***).

You have worked through step 2, the gift. You have given thought to and placed in the forefront of your mind what your gifts and talents are. You recognize the importance of this step, as this pivotal information will most often be used to generate revenue—the revenue needed to make what you envisioned in the next step come to pass. You have completed step 2.

In step 3, you took the time to envision in great detail exactly what you want out of life. You took the time to be intentional in asking the universe to not only supply what you need but you were specific about exactly what you wanted. You can never receive that which you don't ask. You then took it a step further by taking what you envisioned in your mind's eye and made it into a tangible, visual representation of the life you intend to have. You have committed to ponder, mediate on, and visualize your ideal life often; and remember that with each step, your energy must now be dedicated to achieving your goal, your vision. You understand the power that lies within this step and have begun to harness the power of the law of attraction. You have completed step 3, and YOU are ON YOUR WAY! You are on the path to achieving your dreams!

Now faith is the substance of things hoped for, the evidence of things not seen.

—Hebrews 11:1

Faith is the bridge to all dreams.

—Bryant McGill

Faith is taking the first step, even when you don't see the whole staircase.

—MLK

If you have faith the size of a mustard seed, you will say to this mountain, move from here to there and it will move, nothing will be impossible for you.

—Matthew 17:20

Step 4

Faith—Just a Mustard-Seed Size Is All It Takes!

Have you ever planted a seed? You began by gathering what you hoped was fertile soil, full of nutrients and minerals for your plant-to-be. You then placed that soil into a pot that you believed was large enough to allow your plant to flourish. You gathered a handful of seeds and placed it into the soil, just deep enough to be sufficiently covered, but not so deep that your plant won't grow properly. Next, you place that pot in a sunny spot and water it at regular intervals. Each day, you come to water your plant; you check for progress. Each day you visit your seeds, you do so with anticipation and expectation that today, tomorrow, or the following day will be the day you will see a bit of green appear above the top of the soil. Not only do you go to your pot with expectation that the seed will grow, but you presume that it will keep growing until it comes to look very much like the picture on the front of the package of seeds.

In case you did not recognize it as such, growing a plant from a seed to a seedling and then to a full-fledged plant is an exercise in faith. It is an exercise that very much mirrors how you will grow the seed God planted in you when he gave you your vision for your life. If you'll notice when you go to purchase a package of seeds, they all have pictures on them. The packages have pictures of what the seed will become. You begin the process of visualizing your plant before it even leaves the store. You start visualizing before it is even planted or it starts to germinate. You plant the seed in fertile soil—soil that is welcoming to the unrealized potential of the seed it carries, soil that will nourish and take care of the seed as it starts to fulfill its destiny. That soil will give way to the germinating plant as it starts to grow toward the surface and as it develops the necessary root system that it needs for support. You water this yet unrealized potential planted in the soil. You put it in the sun. You may even consult with other experts who have grown this type of plant before—all full well EXPECTING this plant to fulfill its potential. You don't just speak of faith; you exercise faith in your seeds. Remember, faith is the substance of things hoped for, but not yet seen. If you have grown a plant from a package of seeds, you have exercised faith in action. Your vision, the destination for your boat, your destiny, needs the same expectation, the same faith in order to grow.

Your vision needs the same love and care you offer a tiny seed in order to become a reality, in order to blossom and grow from the place deep within you, to become a reality outside of your mind's eye. You have to approach your vision the same way you approach a seed, constantly envisioning the goal. What it will look like once it has grown and blossomed. You must have an unshakable faith that it will blossom, grow, and come to pass. Each time you visit this seed planted deep inside of you, by visualizing your life as you would have it to be, know beyond a shadow of doubt that you are fertile soil. Clear out any rocks of doubt, thoughts of inadequacy, feelings of unworthiness, or anything that tries to weigh you down. Remove any items that will slow down the growth of your vision. Each time you visualize your dream or vision, water it like you would a plant. Research, find out information, about how to obtain a dream like yours—reading a book like this perhaps and remembering and having faith that any day, on one of your visits, you will eventually start to see a little progress and growth with from that seed. You may start to see a little green appear above the soil.

Don't expose your seed to darkness; face it toward the light. Place it somewhere it can get support. You want to continue to speak and breathe life into your vision and nurture it. You would not place your seed in a place where predators can snuff out its existence as soon as it germinates, would you? Just as there are animals eager to dine on a tender, new plant that pushes above the surface of the soil, similar dream-snatchers await the germination of your vision. As sure as you declare and have faith that one day you will (fill in the blank), enemies and obstacles will come against your statement and test your faith. Some of the naysayers and negative Nellys may actually mean well. Aunty So-and-So or your cousin who never saw their dreams come true may feel as though they are protecting you from the hurt they experienced when their dreams and visions did not come to pass. Some actually have your best interest at heart. Others would be negative impactors, hoping to snuff out your vision because of their own perceived inadequacies. They often look like you, are from a similar background as you, and sometimes have the same last name. They can't bring themselves to support and encourage you because that would hold up a mirror to their own station in life. They think to themselves, ***How can a person with a similar starting point as me become as grand as your vision may have you become? How can you become so big while I am still where I am? How dare you? Who do you think you are? You think that you are better,*** etc. And so begins their mission to slowly deter your seed from growing, from germinating. Whenever you speak of the seed inside of you, they make it their business to speak negatively over it and over the possibility of it coming to be. It is your job as the protector of your seed to keep it away from negative exposure. Show your seed THE LIGHT! Don't share something as precious and personal as your vision and your dream for your life with these individuals. You already know who they are because they behaved in the same manner when you shared less important news and goals. This seed is the most important of all—guard it like you would an unborn baby, because it is. It is the ungrown seed to your vision. Did you know that there have been studies that have showed negative impact on plants grown in negative environments? Plants that have had positive, loving owners, who sang to it and/or declared positive statements to the plant showed better growth cycles than those that had the opposite. Negative shouting, declarations, and statements, have been shown to impede plant growth. Do you think that your dream or the vision for your life is any different?

What will be your inner dialogue with your vision, your seedling? Will it be faith-based? Will you speak to it in positives, believing full well in its ability to be exactly what it is destined to be? Do you wholeheartedly believe in your vision and your ability to bring it to life? Sometimes the biggest obstacle we face on the road to our vision is our biggest opponent: OURSELVES. Sometimes it is not a family member or a friend that talks us out of our destiny. Often it is not one particular individual that will convince us that our seed won't grow. We often do it to ourselves. Think about it. Who do you spend the most time with? Why YOU, of course. You are the only one that has access to your innermost, deepest, and darkest thoughts. When you get tired, weary, and want to give up, what is your inner dialogue? How kind have you been to yourself when you have had trouble accomplishing other tasks? What is your inner dialogue when you make a mistake? What about when you fail at your first attempt at a task? Do you break out the Chinese torture devices on yourself? Are you the first one at your own pity party, and then you stay way past the last call at the bar? Do you allow thoughts of inadequacy to replay over and over in your mind until you talk yourself out of accomplishing your goals? If these perceived obstacles have come up before, they will most certainly rear their ugly heads again when you dare to express the faith necessary to work toward your vision. Those heads will be extra ugly too, with really bad weaves on a hot day in July! (Wink, wink.) Just remember that self-reflection and a willingness to simply believe and having faith is the beginning of every dream. All you need to do is to take the first step. Remember, Martin Luther King said that "faith is taking that first step, even though you don't see the full staircase." Faith is believing that God would not place something in you with no plan on how to get you to the destination. You may not know all the people you need to, have all the money necessary, or be as skilled as the person you are comparing yourself to, but your dream is possible. Your seed will grow—all you need to do is envision it fully grown, like on a package of seeds, water it, make sure that its soil is fertile, keep it in the sunlight, and sprinkle it with faith and expectation with each visit.

A woman, who is now famous, was once born into poverty in Mississippi to a teenage mother who gave her away. She was shamed after becoming pregnant and was molested and raped as a young girl. She worked hard and became an anchor on a television show that she eventually was fired from. This seemingly disparaging moment led to a series of events that culminated in her getting her own show, starring in movies, and becoming one of the largest and most famous media icons of our century. She never gave up on the larger-than-life vision she had for her life. She is known as Oprah Winfrey. My bestie in my head (wink, wink).

A well-known Canadian-born gentlemen ended up dropping out of high school after his dad was laid off. He picked up a job as a janitor and a security officer. Unfortunately, these actions still were not enough to keep his family from losing their home. They ended up living in a van, but he kept the faith. He believed in himself and what he wanted from life. He eventually moved to America, auditioned for ***In Living Color***, and the rest is history. His name is Jim Carrey. He is living out his dream.

This gentleman spent the early years of his life in Charleston, West Virginia, taking care of his ill father and dropping out of college. He answered his call to be a minister, but it would be decades before he would become a household name. He worked at a local factory, met his wife, and started a family all while working as a part-time minister. He eventually decided to go all in as a pastor and focused on building his church, which moved locations several times. He eventually began a Sunday school series, which became a cornerstone of his work and later became a book and then a movie—***Woman, Thou Art Loosed.*** This world-renown pastor toiled and had faith in his vision, and it is the reason we know who he is today. He is a prolific writer with over thirty books published and the pastor of the famous Potter's house church in Dallas, Texas. He is Pastor T. D. Jakes.

Another person who started out in life just as small, or even smaller than many who have lived their lives to the fullest, began her life in St. Louis at the height of segregation. She bounced through as many professions as you can think of—a cook, a cable car operator, a dancer, an actor, a writer, a professor, and a poet. She eventually became one of the most prolific and celebrated authors of all time. She has won a Grammy and was awarded the Presidential Medal of Freedom. She was born Marguerite Annie Johnson, better known as Maya Angelou.

You may say to yourself that you are happy for and may have been blessed by something that the aforementioned individuals have done or been a part of; but you are no Oprah, Jim Carrey, T. D. Jakes, or Maya Angelou. If you have come to this conclusion, you are absolutely right! You aren't anyone but you, and your vision, no matter how grand, may not involve anything even remotely close to what we know these individuals for. This fact, however, does not negate the fact that your vision is possible. The individuals that were mentioned above were discussed as just a few of millions of stories like theirs—people who have overcome tremendous odds, people who have powered themselves over roadblocks, setups, and setbacks. These individuals were able to do so because when all else failed, when the chips were down and they may have wanted to give up, they kept the faith. When things looked the most bleak, when they were weary and wanted to throw in the towel and just slip back into the fold of the ordinary, they mustered up just enough gumption and FAITH to go just a little bit farther. They believed that even though their seed may not have sprouted exactly on the same day as someone else's, they continued to believe in its potential. They kept envisioning, they kept watering, and they kept visiting and working toward their dream with expectation. They knew the importance of step 4: FAITH! They made sure they kept a measure of at least one mustard seed. They knew that FAITH was the key, and now so do you!

The distance between dreams and
reality is called ACTION.

—Unknown

Action is the foundational key to all success.

—Pablo Picasso

Take action! An inch of movement
will bring you closer to your goals,
than a mile of intention.

—Steve Maraboli

Step 5

Implementation—Get to It!

You are awake. You have a specific vision of what you want your life to be, and you have faith that you are capable of bringing that dream to fruition. But James 2:14 says that "faith without works is dead." Meaning that wanting a change, visualizing exactly what you want, having faith that you can get there, and then rolling over and taking a nap and waiting for God to deliver it to your doorstep will result in your vision being dead in the water! That is like planting a seed, picturing it growing into the plant that you saw on the package, and then never taking the time to water or tend to the plant to ensure that it grows as intended. Who would think that this would work? No one, of course! However, this step, IMPLEMENTATION, is where many a dream goes to die.

Many people can tell you specifically what they would possess and what they would do if they could have the exact life they wished for. These same folks often can't tell you what they are doing on a regular basis to help move themselves closer to achieving that vision. There are plenty of individuals that see the big picture, the end result, and the vision but are unable to see small steps that they can take to help get them there. Individuals falsely believe they have to be able to connect all the dots, know all the individuals necessary, be approved for the big loan, etc. before they can even get started. They believe the timing needs to be perfect and they need to have all their ducks in a row. As soon as so-and-so goes to kindergarten or when they get the promotion, as soon as they are able to save this amount of money or can move to this location, THEN they'll start working on (fill in the dream/vision here). Herein lies why so many people never get to see their dream come to fruition.

A very common colloquial, but true statement that I heard quite a bit as a child was "If it ain't one thing, it's another." In relation to going after your dreams, this means that the road will **NEVER**, **EVER** be completely clear! Life is not going to stop happening because you have suddenly awakened. Life does not pause like a video game because you suddenly realize that you have a vision and you finally want to make changes in your life to move toward it. Usually, it is quite the opposite. The reality is that it seems as though when you set your mind to accomplish a goal or move toward your vision, life happens at a more furious pace. Your car breaks down, your kids start having trouble in school, your marriage is on the rocks, you have to move suddenly, you break your foot—on and on and on. As soon as you decide you are going to use the law of attraction to your benefit, don't believe for one second that your desired life will suddenly hit you in the face and you'll live happily ever after!

The one thing that many don't realize though is that life is happening to ALL of us. We get stuck in our own heads that we are all alone in the fury of life. However, if you quiz those around you, each person, no matter what their perceived level of success is, they are all in a storm of their own. They may not be dealing with your specific issue, but they most certainly are dealing with one of their own. The sun rises and the rain falls on **ALL** of us. We all have a cross to bear. Maybe it's insecurity. The person in the cubicle next to you at work could be a recovering addict, struggling with their weight or their health. Even though your boss makes more than you, he or she may be dealing with financial instability or just getting out of a toxic relationship. We all have ups and downs. The difference maker between those who are able to live out their dreams and vision for their lives and those who never make it to that point is what the successful do while life is happening to them. They take the steps toward their vision **ANYWAY**! They make time to take steps toward their dreams through all the chaos that may be swirling around them. It's all about **ACTION**! Those who are successful at living the life they envision know that there NEVER will be a perfect time. They realize that they can take the first five steps toward their goals even though they don't know exactly what to do for steps 6 through 10. It is OK to start small and grow into the vision that you have in your head; in fact, it is often necessary! Just because you don't know all the steps to being the businessman that Magic Johnson is, or you don't know the steps to starting your restaurant empire or filling an art gallery with your works, does not mean you can't take one or two steps in that direction.

In the beginning of each school year, teachers all across the United States are given a digital or a hardcopy of a set of standards that they must teach their students by the end of the school year. These standards are specific topics their students must master by a set date later in the year in order for them to be prepared for state-mandated testing. The testing that most students take in May or June is designed to measure their mastery of the standards they were to be focused on during the school year. Once teachers are given these standards, they are asked to work backward and design steps in which they will use to get students to the goal. The goal is for students to master the standards, do well during testing, and be prepared for the next grade. In the education world, this is called backwards design. You look at a goal and work backward, designing small incremental steps to reach that goal.

The first thing a good teacher does in the beginning of the year is to take stock as to where his or her students are at that time. How much background knowledge do they come to the class with? Teachers do this so that they will know where they need to start in order to get the students to their goal. If they teach first grade, are they starting with students who are beginning readers, or will they have to teach them letter sounds or the concept of a letter altogether? If you were going to teach someone to cook, have they cooked a few meals previously or is boiling water an accomplishment? These are important things to know when you want to teach someone something. You need to know where to start. Once a teacher has this information, they can add or subtract steps from their plan and proceed through the steps they have designed to get students to the goal. The concept of backwards design is not just relegated to the educational field. Some form of this method is used by every individual that is successful at reaching the life they envision, and it can be used by you as well. This is where your IMPLEMENTATION, your ACTION, will begin!

What are the talents and gifts that you established in step 2? Are you a phenomenal educator, a talented barber, a great cook, or an artist? What is the vision for your life that you established in step 3? Did you envision yourself living in a custom-built home, running a homeless shelter, and having more time and money to travel? Whatever your talents or gifts were in step 2, during the implementation phase, we have to connect them to your vision and put together a plan of actionable steps to help you to reach it. Ta-da! Backwards design!

Talents + Implementation Steps = Your Vision for Your Life

Here we go! Again, we will go back to what you established your talents were and think about how we will connect them to your vision. Maybe you have already done this. Perhaps you are a talented hairdresser and your vision includes having a multimillion dollar hairline. Or you a scientist and your vision entails you coming up with a new pharmaceutical or drug that will help cure cancer. Perhaps you are tech savvy and your vision involves you starting your own tech firm. If your vision is already connected to your talents and gifts, awesome! However, for some, that may not always be the case. Someone reading this book may have been an educator for some years and want to open their own restaurant or maybe a truck driver who wants to own a lawn-care service as a part of their vision. Or perhaps you've worked in the banking industry and no longer want to work a traditional nine-to-five anymore and want to get into real estate. No matter what your vision is, as long as you still plan to reside on this planet, you will need to continue to generate income. The goal, however, is to be able to do so in a way that is in line with your talents and the vision you have for your life. Regardless as to whether your talent is inherently connected to your vision or not, you can follow the actionable steps below toward your ideal life.

Implementation Step 1: Assess

Your first step needs to be to assess what you know about your overall goal. If you want to run an addiction clinic, start an architectural firm, or open a supermarket, what is your baseline knowledge about what you need to do to reach this goal? Remember the term ***backwards design***? Remember, the first step was for the teacher to assess where his/her students were in the beginning of the year. The teacher needed to assess where the students were so they would know where to start teaching. Which standards does he or she cover first? A chef can't start with teaching you the nuances of poaching eggs perfectly if you don't know how to turn on the stovetop. In your case, you need to assess how much knowledge you have already about your end goal so you know where to fill in the gaps.

Implementation Step 2: Acquire Information

Once your figure out what you do know about your overall goal, your next step is to research and gather as much information as possible about your goal. Fill in the gaps in your knowledge base. Today, this is a relatively easy step. Most people have access to a computer or a smartphone. You have access to information twenty-four hours a day, seven days a week. If you don't currently possess a smartphone, all public libraries across the United States allow the public access to the internet. All you need to do is fill out a brief application for a library card. Use the internet to research websites, articles, and books about your end goal. If you want to open a catering company or a bounce house, look up as much information as you can about doing so. How many businesses, organizations, or offices near you are similar to the one that you would like to start or work for? Look at their marketing materials, websites, and events that these businesses hold to sustain their businesses or organizations. Is there a small business administration office near you where you can get information? What steps will you need to take to establish such a business or organization in your state, county, and city? If your goal entails specialized training, which schools in your area offer the training you seek? How much does it cost, and do they offer financial aid? How long will it take for you to acquire what you need to get licensed, certificated, or certified? Find out as much information as possible. You want to be as knowledgeable as possible about what you plan to embark on.

Implementation Step 3: Seek Out Mentorship

Have you ever heard the saying "There is nothing new under the sun"? It's such a popular saying, because there really isn't. That idea that you have, as awesome as it may be, is not totally original. There is someone within driving distance from you that has a similar business or is operating a similar organization. This is not to be taken as an insult, nor does it mean that your idea, your talent, or your gift can't be used in your area to lead you to the life that you envision for yourself and your family. It actually means quite the opposite. If someone near you has operated a daycare center, hardware store, church, or something similar to what you want to do, that means your success is possible as well. Use the internet. Look up a few of these businesses or organizations near you. If possible, find a similar organization/business that is not in the same area in which you believe that you will do business (if it is a business you seek). This way, once you actually get to speak to someone they won't feel threatened. Ask to speak to the owner. Tell them that you are doing research and you need to interview a person like them to complete your project. If your dream does not entail opening a business, then this step is even easier for you. Simply find someone near you that already has the job, holds the position, or is doing what you aspire to. If you are on the downward side of your career and are looking at retirement and enjoying your later years, speak with someone already in the thick of retirement. Ask them what they wish they knew when they retired and what advice they wish they had when they were in your position. No matter what your end goal is, the objective is to get to speak to a few real people on the path you are beginning to embark on. At the very least, the individual can fill in the "I wish I would have known" information you may miss while doing your own personal research. You don't have to develop the type of relationship that has your mentor at your house for Thanksgiving, but ideally you should hope to build a relationship that will facilitate them advising you as you travel along your path.

Implementation Step 4: Go

Go forth and prosper, my child! Well, actually, it's not quite that simple; otherwise, the book would end here, and as you can see, there are quite a few pages left. However, the first word in implementing step 4 is applicable: GO! Get going, get moving. You have enough knowledge after implementation steps 1 to 3 to do SOMETHING. If you need to take a class, sign up. Planning for retirement and need to up continue to diversify your portfolio? Do so. You find out that you need to buy some additional supplies to start your all natural health and beauty line? Purchase them. If you discover that some of the things you need to fully implement your goal or use your talent require funding that you don't have, start saving and start small. Let me say it again for the people in the back: Start SAVING and start SMALL! Set up a separate bank account that you can't see every time you log in to your online account to save for your startup funds. Using a separate bank might even be a good idea. Why, you ask? Because out of sight, out of mind. This account won't be out of sight if you see the money building every time you check your main accounts. What you don't want is to see your new vision account as a separate savings fund that you can dip into if a perceived emergency strikes. Once you set up the account, set up automatic deposits to the account until you reach your goal. DO NOT TOUCH THESE FUNDS unless you have an extreme emergency. As in, you are literally about to be tossed out on the street with nowhere to go or your car breaks down and you have no other way to get it fixed and you will lose your job. You need to pretend that these funds don't exist as they build. Go about your life and do what you would do to live day to day if you really didn't have the vision savings account. If you don't operate in this manner, and your vision requires funding, you will never reach your goal account balance. Because, remember, life won't stop because you have a goal. "If it ain't one thing, it's another" will still be true. Your new account can't be your go-to whenever life happens.

What should you do while you continue to build your savings? Well, this is where the start-small part comes in. If you need a barber's license to open the massive barbershop you have in mind but you are still saving, what is stopping you from building your clientele now? What are the restrictions on you offering mobile barbering in your area until you save enough to open your shop? Want to open that restaurant? What do you need to do to run a legitimate catering business or lunch-delivery service in your area? You can slowly get your name out in the community by doing church functions and delivering boxed lunches to schools and offices near you and build your business that way. Want to start your own recording studio? What is stopping you from slowly getting padding, mixers, etc. to turn a room in your home into a small studio? You can advertise at open mic nights to up-and-comers and offer them a discounted rate. The point is, no matter what your ultimate goal is, there is a scaled-down version of it that you can start NOW. Everything does not have to be perfect. You don't have to know all the ins and outs. You don't have to wait until you get 100k, 50k, or even 5,000 in your vision account to get started. Once you have complete implementation steps 1 to 3, you can easily start step 4.

After you complete implementation steps 1 to 4, your path will differ depending on your specific dream or vision. However, whatever you do next, it should be a natural, gradual, and calculated extension of what you accomplished in steps 1 to 4. You will continue to cycle through these steps again and again as you plan your next steps. As you get going, continue to educate yourself, consult with those in the know, and save and exercise sound financial decisions. Doing so will make it possible to fund your vision as your move toward it.

The only thing at this point between you and the beginning phases of reaching your vision is your dedication and willingness to follow the process. If you have gotten this far, you have battled through a good portion of the steps needed to reach your vision. Keep on your battle gear though. There are still a few more hurdles to cross. But so far, soldier, you've done well. The Promised Land is just over the hill. Just keep climbing. We are about halfway there.

Everything you want is on
the other side of fear.

—Jack Canfield

Fear kills more dreams than failure ever will.

—Suzy Kassem

So do not fear, for I am with you; do not
be dismayed, for I am your God. I will
strengthen you and help you; I will uphold
you with my righteous right hand.

—Isaiah 41:10

The phrase "Do not be afraid" is written 365
times in the Bible. That is a daily reminder
from God to live everyday being fearless.

—Unknown

Step 6

Don't Let Fear Win

The chapter on fear really could have been placed anywhere after chapter 1 in this book because fear almost always accompanies the unknown. As soon as you make the decision to take steps toward something you have never had or done before, without a doubt, one of the first emotions that will creep into your psyche is fear. It is a frequent and normal response to feel uneasy about the unknown. You are planning to embark on something that you have never done before. You are opting to travel a road that will lead to dreams and a vision that most won't dare to reach for. The road less traveled does not have as many footsteps to follow, so it is natural to feel uneasy as you set out on this journey. But this natural human response can be conquered. In fact, you have already previously conquered fear, and you can conquer your fears again and again, as many times as you need to reach your goal.

Think back some years ago. For some who are like myself, we have to think back a little further (wink wink!). Remember when you were in school? Do you remember kindergarten, middle school, and high school? Do you remember the thoughts that that accompanied those new experiences? You thought to yourself, ***Do I know enough? Will I make friends? Will I be able to do well? Will I enjoy this new experience?***

What about when you transitioned to a new job, obtained a new position, or moved to a new area. The same uneasiness and fear reemerged. ***Will I make friends? Will I be able to find my way? Will I catch on fast enough? Will I be able to advance? Will I like it here?*** You see, you have been conquering fear your whole life. You just may not have realized it because, as we grow and develop, fear changes disguises to match where you are in life. I mean, how effective could fear be if it didn't? What scared you at three certainly won't scare you at ten, right? Well, except for those few adults that are still scared of the dark (hey, no judgment here . . . wink, wink). Let's elaborate and make your previous slaying of fear plain.

Your first encounter with fear probably came when you first learned to walk. You sat there watching everyone around you walk around on their feet, running, jumping, and playing; and you thought to yourself, ***I want to do that.*** So you gave it a shot. On your first attempt, you were probably a bit wobbly and most likely you fell. That tumble probably was unexpected and made you nervous. Walking was not as easy as it looked, and if you scraped your knee or bumped your head, the pain of the event gave you your first taste of fear. You thought, ***Whoa! That was unpleasant, that hurt!*** Fear at this point in your life, if you can imagine, was probably pint-sized. Probably about as small as you were. How big did fear need to be to scare a baby? But guess what? Even as scary as fear was at that point, as many times as you fell and hurt yourself, you kept trying. You worked past your fear of falling and hurting yourself. You did so because the freedom, the reward, of walking, running, and playing meant more to you than the fear of falling and hurting yourself. You conquered fear before you could even say the word ***fear***!

By the time you got to grade school, fear had become a bit more sophisticated. He dressed himself as shadows in a dark room, creaks in the floor, those weird noises in the basement, and what you imagined would be waiting for you on your first day of school. All unknowns and new adventures. Guess what? You conquered those too!

As an adult, you have already conquered monstrous, giant, big, ugly, as scary as they can be fears. You moved away from your family to make your way in a new city or state. You went into the military and made it through AIT and basic training. You began the journey into single parenting and all it entails. You got a divorce and started a new life. You began a new career. You left the nest and went off to college. You quit a job that was making your miserable. You picked up the pieces of your broken heart after a failed relationship or the loss of a loved one. Although most have not had **ALL** the experiences that were just outlined, most have experienced a few or at least can relate.

Now that we have helped you remember your previous victories over fear, let me introduce you to my friend Mike. Mike started life in the average American family, with its share of ups and downs. There were times of feast and times of famine in his family, just like most families. Mike was an average student in school; however, when you spoke to Mike, he had some pretty large dreams for his life. Mike's dreams would require him to master fear and live outside of what he'd known and become accustomed to. Mike had plans to go off to college, start his own business, become a millionaire, and take his piece of the American dream and then some.

While in high school, Mike got a job at McDonalds at sixteen. He was a reliable employee, but he had plans to make it big after graduation. He applied to a few local colleges and got in, but he could not figure out how to pay for it. He was offered an opportunity to study abroad, an opportunity that, at its conclusion, would help him pay for college; but the journey was to some foreign land he knew nothing about. The unknown equaled fear. Mike decided against it. Instead, he planned to work for a year, save, and go to college after. During the year after Mike graduated from high school, he spoke about his dreams often and still had plans to make it big. He bought a car and was offered the opportunity take an internship at a corporation that could lead to a scholarship for college. The internship would require that Mike work in a field that he had not yet trained for. They expected him to learn as he went. How was he supposed to learn and meet performance quotas? More unknowns. Plus, he would have to leave his job at McDonalds. Mike, as well as those around him, thought that those were crazy expectations, so he turned it down. He reasoned that it wasn't a big deal because he was saving to pay for school while he was working at McDonalds. By now, Mike had been at McDonalds for three years and was promoted to shift supervisor. It was a fancier title than cashier, more responsibility, but not much more money. It also had the lure of predictability; it was in Mike's comfort zone. No unknowns, nothing to fear. But it was still a far cry from the dreams Mike had spoke so often about. Fast forward a few years later, two kids and a wife later. Mike did not take advantage of multiple opportunities to further his education or to advance at McDonalds that took him outside his comfort zone. He never admitted it, but his fears were keeping him from achieving his dreams. He still spoke of his dreams and plans, but as time went on, his conversations became peppered with a more negative tone and pointed discussion of those who were responsible for him not reaching his goals just yet.

You may not know my friend Mike, but you certainly know someone just like Mike. Or maybe you don't know Mike because you . . . are . . . MIKE. That is not a horrible thing. Mike is not a bad person. He got up every day and worked for a living, just like the next guy. He was not looking for a handout. However, in his young age, he had already developed a habit that if he wasn't careful would help him to live out the rest of his life <u>NEVER</u> being able to accomplish his dreams. Anytime Mike was faced with the unknown or obstacles that were outside of the realm of what he'd already been accustomed to or experienced, Mike backed down. He turned away from opportunities that could have helped him achieve the life he'd been dreaming of. He didn't turn away from these opportunities with the intent of not achieving his dreams; he turned away out of fear.

Now if you know a Mike, are related to someone like him, or you are the Mike in the story above, don't dismay. As sure as you are reading these words, you can make the decision not to be Mike anymore. Mike didn't realize that he was responsible for delaying his dreams; delays he was responsible, all because of fear—fear of new experiences, new demands, and new expectations. If you are not Mike overall, we all have had Mike-like situations. We have all shied away from situations that would make us uncomfortable or stretch and grow us in ways that we have not been accustomed to previously. But the only way to graduate from where you are now to the vision that you have for your life is to stretch and reach toward it. If faced with two logical next steps, one that is comfortable and one that will stretch you and scares you a bit, reach for the scary one. That is how you defeat fear and grow into the person worthy of the life and vision that you seek. With each choice to work through fear and defeat it, fear will get smaller and smaller. It will no longer be a worthy opponent. It will NOT stop you from living out the life of your dreams.

This journey that you are now on is going to test you and try you in ways that you have never experienced. At times you will want to go back to what you know. There is comfort in the familiar. The same old people and situations that you have already mastered. Just know that each time you do, you will be acting like Mike. It won't be like the old "be like Mike" Nike Michael Jordan commercials either. You won't reach the pinnacle of greatness like Michael Jordan. The end result of mirroring the behavior of the Mike in this chapter will get you the same results he received—dreams delayed and deferred indefinitely.

Now we know what comes next, don't we? The questions, the excuses, we use to justify us behaving like Mike. What if you strike out on this journey and you can't make it work? What if you can't save enough money for your restaurant in the next year or so? What if you don't get into the premier school in the field of your dreams? What if, what if, WHAT IF! Do you know how many what-ifs there are attached to your specific dream or vision? An infinite amount! For everything that could go the way you want it to, there are a billion things that could go in the opposite direction. In fact, I could write an entire chapter on all the things that could go wrong. But I have a few specific what-ifs that I'm much more interested in. What if, after a few attempts, things work out? What if, despite it all, you make it? What if you fight through the people and situations that would have normally turned you around, and you prevail! What if, on this side of heaven, you get to live out life as you envision it! I know that I would rather fail at trying to be extraordinary than to prevail at being average!

Now I'm not going to lie to you. It's not going to be an easy process. Fear is big, ugly, and fierce. It has robbed many a man and woman of their dreams and visions for their lives. You are going to run up against obstacles and delayed victories, cloaked in present failures. But you have to PUSH THROUGH. You will have to keep trying and keep working. Beat fear down until it doesn't have the bite it once had. Wrestle with it until you get so accustomed to its patterns that it becomes predictable. Remember when you were younger and played video games? You played them so much that you started to be able to anticipate the bad guy's moves and react before they even started to attack. You were able to time, anticipate, and eventually defeat the enemy. By the time you reach your vision, you will have become so familiar with fear and how to defeat it, it will be like that video game villain. You'll be able to time its moves as well as defeat it with ease. Fear will not win. Your dreams and vision for your life will PREVAIL!

The only thing sadder than the willingness of hateful people to drag us down to their level is our willingness to oblige.

—Dr. Steve Maraboli

Don't be a victim of negative self-talk. Remember YOU are listening.

—Bob Proctor

Surround yourself with people who encourage you, inspire you, and believe in your dreams.

—Roger James

There will always be rocks in the road ahead of us. They will be stumbling blocks or stepping stones; it all depends on how you use them.

—Friedrich Nietzsche

Step 7

The Traps (Detractors, Negative Self-Talk, and Box Dwellers, Oh My!)

Picture yourself about to begin a race. As you approach the start line, you look into the stands at your cheering section. How fortunate you are to have so many supporters! They are even wearing matching T-shirts that say "Go, [insert your name], GO!" Now imagine that for every ten people that you have cheering for you, you have one to two people that are not so happy about your journey. The only problem is that those individuals are interspersed within the approximately fifty people cheering for you; the secret haters are there also, wearing the same smiles and T-shirts as those who are genuinely cheering you on. On the outside, they appear to support you, just the same as the others; but under the microscope, they are very, VERY different.

Guess what? The scenario that was just painted for you is very much like the endeavor that you are about to embark on, except the stakes are higher and the payoff is many times greater. You have decided to make a change and ***awakened*** from your slumber. You have discovered your ***talents and gifts***. You are doing the work required to align your new thought process with actionable ***implementation*** **steps**, and you are using ***faith*** to help push yourself forward and power you through the tough times that are sure to come. Last but not least, you are diligently working to keep ***fear*** in its place and out of your way! You know that you still have quite a distance to go before you make the life of your dreams a reality, but how great it is to be working on your dreams instead of those of the CEO of the company your work!

You know that the road ahead will have a few bumps in it, but you are up for the challenge. Wouldn't it be great, though, if you could anticipate some of those bumps? You know that you are not going to wake up tomorrow with your own personal crystal ball on your dresser (if you do, holler at your girl! Wink, wink!). It would, however, be nice if you could anticipate some of the issues that you may face on this path so that you can avoid getting hung up on them. This takes us back to the race you were starting a couple paragraphs ago and the secret haters cheering you on from the stands. Well, guess what? At this minute, you probably aren't standing outside with this book in your hand about to start a marathon. Running a marathon while reading requires talents that neither of us probably has! However, that does not mean the analogy at the beginning of this chapter does not apply to you, your neighbor, and pretty much every other person that sets out to change their lives. The race that was alluded to a few paragraphs ago is very much like the journey you are committing to in order to make your dreams and vision for your life a reality. As you get ready to embark on the path to fulfilling your dreams, I'm going to let you in on a not-so-big, not-so-secret, SECRET. Guess what? There are snakes in your midst! Not actual snakes. If I'm wrong about that, RUN! I can't help you read your way out of the grips of an actual snake, but we can discuss the figurative ones—the snakes, the backstabbers, the haters. Anyone that has lived long enough to understand the words in this book have experienced and have dealt with them. That's why the 1970s soul classic "Backstabbers," performed by ***The Ojays*** was, and still is, such a popular and relatable song. "They smile in your face, / all the while, they wanna take your place. / The backstabbers, BACKSTABBERS!"

Every adult I know can name a few. Someone that they thought had their back. Someone that they thought wanted the best for them.

They were in the stands, like in our analogy. They even bought the T-shirt "Go, [insert your name], go!" They are your classmate, your coworker, your cousin, your sister, your brother, and sometimes they are even closer than that! They cheer you on while in front of you, then talk negatively about you and/or try to sabotage you when you are not around. This is an example of what could be a roadblock on the way to your ideal existence that you can potentially foresee and avoid. Even though the current, or would-be haters, near you are wearing the T-shirt and carrying the pom-poms, they are easy to spot when you know what to look for. These are individuals that you need to distance yourself and your dream/vision from. Don't tell them about your dreams, vision, or any plans you have that relate to it. If you do, they will do what they are programmed to do. They will try to discourage you or turn you away from your path. Some of your haters, discouragers, and saboteurs are conscious of their ways; others are not. Don't spend an ounce of your energy trying to change them or figure them out. You'll need all your efforts to power yourself toward your dreams! All you need to do is know how to spot them and keep them away from your seedling—your vision—that you are trying to get to flourish.

So how do you see the forest through the trees? How do you spot a hater, especially one that probably is and has been right under your nose, you ask? One easy way to spot them is you watch those around you and their behavior toward others. Haters and saboteurs usually don't have just one prime target. They will reveal themselves by displaying their backstabbing behavior toward someone else. A genuine person is a genuine person. They are usually consistent. Guess what? Haters are consistent too. Do you have individuals in your midst that smile and pretend to be loving and supportive when around certain individuals and then talk negatively about those same individuals behind their back? If you watch these suspected backstabbers long enough and see that this behavior is consistent with multiple individuals they interact with, how do you think they speak of you when you are not around?

Another way to spot a hater is that a person is simply very negative ALL THE TIME. How can an extremely negative person be anything BUT a hater? A miserable person will obsess about how crappy the weather was two days ago, rather than enjoy the sunshine today. This type of person certainly is not going to help you look on the bright side when the chips are down or when you hit a roadblock and need help or advise as you move toward your dreams.

Why do these haters do what they do? Sometimes its learned behavior, mimicked and passed down from negative people they grew up around. Sometimes it is caused by the individual's own insecurities or childhood traumas. Other times, it is because they can't see themselves achieving or having what those around them have or are striving for, so they tear them down. It's easier for a negative person to discourage and disparage, rather than to get out of their comfort zone and believe in themselves enough to work toward their own aspirations. Hear this LOUD AND CLEAR: It is not your job to fix them though, no matter how close to you your secret haters are. It is also not your job to spend an ounce of energy outing them, arguing with them, confronting them, or anything else that will take valuable energy or time away from achieving your vision for your life. Your job is to recognize them, stay away from them, and don't give them the opportunity to throw a monkey wrench in your plans or to put real or imaginary obstacles in your path. Protect your vision and your dreams from their negativity. Don't confide in them, don't ask them for support, and make your moves in silence when it comes to identified haters and backstabbers.

You need to surround yourself with people who will sow positivity and encouragement you way. When you get discouraged, hit a wall, or are running low on faith, you need someone that will breathe life back into you, not rob you of what, at the moment, may feel like your last breath.

But what if you have done a good job of taking out the trash? What about when you have gotten rid of or distanced yourself from the haters and backstabbers? Who are you left with then?

Who do you spend most of your time with? Who has unprecedented access to your inner most-private thoughts? Who is there with you when the chips are up, down, and everywhere in between? Who is there with you in the midnight hour when everyone is sleep, and you have no one else to talk to? I'm not talking about your parents, your children, or your significant other. Who in the natural world fits this description? If you have not guessed it by now, the answer is—YOU! Once you distance yourself from others, there is one person that you can't escape from, and that is YOU! When you are alone with your thoughts, what do your thoughts consist of? Do you like yourself? Are you as kind and forgiving with yourself as you are with other people? What is your inner dialogue like? How will you talk to yourself as you embark on this journey? How do you currently speak to yourself? You ever heard the expression "You are your worst enemy"? Does that expression describe you? Will you be one of your own speedbumps on the road to your vision for your life?

The questions posed in the previous paragraph are very important ones. They are questions that must be examined and explored if you are to reach your goal of living the life you dream of. Once you rid yourself of other individuals who may try to derail your progress, you will still have trouble living the life you strive for if you are just as discouraging to yourself as they were.

Again, what is your inner dialogue with yourself? Do you know how to pick yourself up and encourage yourself? Before you look to your parent, sibling, friend, or significant other, when the chips are down, what do you say to yourself? Do you know how to find the silver lining? Do you know how to practice positive phrasing when you are faced with a difficult situation? Do you say positive things to and about yourself?

Meet Phylicia and Dawn. Phylicia and Dawn went to grade school together and have been friends for a very long time; in fact, if they were a pair of teenagers, they would probably refer to themselves as besties. While in college, both ladies kissed their share of frogs and fell into and out of relationships as young people tend to do, but Phylicia always believed that she would find her soulmate. Dawn didn't think it was impossible to find her soulmate; she just wasn't absolutely sure it was something that would happen for her. These two ladies went about most of their lives in the same manner. Phylicia seemingly more of an optimist, believing that most things that were out there for some, were also there for her, if she really wanted them. Dawn didn't necessarily think otherwise, but she didn't have the faith that she could hold anything she could conceive in her mind, one day in her hand. Based on the introduction that was given about these ladies, you could guess how their inner dialogue differed. Both women eventually became physicians and were struggling with their next steps in life. Both knew what it was that they felt would bring them greater peace, joy, and happiness and discussed those things frequently. When Phylicia spoke about her quest to start her own practice as well as start a family, she always spoke as if it was already in the works. She would say things like "Dawn, in the next two years when I open my practice" or "I've been looking at spaces and financing options for my business." Her dialogue would also include statements like "I just know that things will line up soon. I've just got to keep putting in the work." Or she'd say things like "I know that the man of my dreams is out there. If my parents found each other, then a love like theirs is in the cards for me too!" Dawn, on the other hand, had a tendency not to be quite so optimistic. She wasn't exactly negative, but her dialogue to and about herself was not as kind. While speaking with Phylicia, she'd say things like "Phylicia, I wish I was as driven as you. It will probably take me another five to ten years to get my own practice, if I'm fortunate." She also said to Phylicia, "Your parents are so cute to watch. The love they have for each other fills a room. One day, if I'm fortunate, hopefully I can find a man like your dad." In examining these two friends, there is nothing that Dawn said that makes her a negative Nelly; however, in order for her to reach her maximum potential, she will need to retrain herself to speak in positive affirmations about and to herself.

What does it mean to speak in positive affirmations to yourself? It means speak your wants and the vision you are striving for into existence. Talk about the children and loving spouse you will have. Talk about WHEN you start your business, not ***IF*** you are able to start it. Declare how you will live once you are financially free, not IF you can ever get from under your debt. Speak about and to yourself like Phylicia, not Dawn. If you have already made a habit of saying negative things or unkind things about yourself out loud, it is a habit you can and need to break. On your journey, you will need positive people to cheer you on and help you when you fall. Who better than YOU to fill this role? But you won't be a good cheerleader for yourself if you don't master having a positive dialogue to and about yourself. Start with practicing changing the way you phrase things you say about yourself and your journey out loud. Practice not saying negative things about yourself and your journey when speaking to others. Instead of saying "I wish I could find a house as nice as yours in my price range," say "I know that the house of my dreams is out there, and I'll find it soon." Instead of "I hope that one day I can get to open that restaurant I've been dreaming of," say "I'm working on gaining the knowledge and resources to open my own successful restaurant. I want to open it within the next year and a half." As Maya Angelou once alluded to, she believed that words were things. She said that they get into the carpet and get on the walls. Words are more powerful than people give them credit for. For that reason, practice using your words and thoughts to help power your dreams, not crush them. The Bible says that life and death lie in THE TONGUE!

Once you work on what comes out of your mouth, move to mastering what bounces between your ears. Master your inner dialogue. When you have a delayed victory or a lesson learned, see it as just that. Every failure is simply you narrowing the field so that you can find the right path. You now have crossed off one more path that won't work. Now on to test the next path. Each time you don't get it right, you are one step closer to the right path, the right answer. Instead of getting down and speaking negatively about the experience, look at the situation and examine what you can learn. What is the takeaway that can be applied to your continued journey to the life of your dreams? As long as you stay on the path toward your vision, there aren't any mistakes. Perceived ***mistakes*** are delayed victories or lessons learned. See them as such. Don't waste time and energy beating yourself up. Be as kind and forgiving to yourself as you are to others. When a temporary roadblock we have not discussed in this chapter appears, see it as such and take your time and figure out how to get around it.

So you've read everything above, and it sounds great, right? But what about when you have a bad day? It is unrealistic to believe that you are going to read this book, change a few things about the way you speak about and regard yourself internally, and then become "Sally or Billy smiles a lot," right? You are not, all of a sudden, going to start burping butterflies and pooping rainbows (wink, wink). Of course not, but practice makes perfect. Make sure that once you have a crappy day, you don't allow it to roll over into a crappy few days, a crappy week, etc. Sit in dismay momentarily. Don't set up camp there! Don't derail your own progress. Be your own cheerleader. Speak well of yourself, your dreams, your aspirations, and your vision. Master your inner dialogue, and you will be able to remain on the path to achieving the life you are striving for.

No matter how long this chapter is, it is not possible to anticipate every possible roadblock, distraction, and obstacle that may try to get in your way before you reach your goal. We've already discussed the haters, as well as your responsibility in maintaining a positive inner dialogue as you take this journey. We also spoke about acknowledging and recognizing the power of your words. These are all very important things to be mindful of, but we would be remiss if we did not mention one more trap to look out for—and that is the box dwellers in your life. Now you are probably scratching your head trying to figure out just what a box dweller is. As weird as it sounds, they are exactly what it sounds like. They are individuals who have lived a good portion of their lives scared to get out of their own comfortable box, their comfort zone. We all have them around us. They are not necessarily bad people; however, they can be dream killers if you allow them to be. These individuals have lived a good portion of their lives at one station in life. Because of the amount of time they have spent at this station, they sometimes have a hard time thinking outside of the comfortable box that they have created for themselves. These individuals often not only limit themselves but they also have a hard time thinking outside of the box for those around them. Again, these are not bad people, they just are not the ones you want to confide in or seek out when you need encouragement. Because they have resided so long on the ground- or midlevel of the forest, they will have a hard time encouraging you to fly above the trees. At the very least, they won't be very encouraging; at their worst, they can be masters at recruiting you to come to live and get comfortable in the box with them.

Friends and relatives living in a box often want company. They often have a hard time thinking outside of the realm of what they perceive as possible for them. They will encourage you not to fly too high, not to dream so big, and not to strive for too much. If you listen long enough, they will have you doubting yourself and whether your dream and vision for your life is even possible, clipping your wings little by little with each conversation. Recognize the box dwellers around you and refrain from discussing your journey with them.

Remember, you are now on the path that leads to the life you envision for yourself. Your path, no matter where it specifically leads to, will have roadblocks and would-be detours. Although we have spent this chapter cautioning you and preparing you for very common roadblocks and challenges faced by those on a journey similar to you, we can't possibly anticipate it all. What you can and should do is take this chapter to heart, expect challenges, and ready yourself with the right mindset to overcome them. Remember that if you can conceive it you can achieve it. Many have come before you and many will follow. Your dreams and vision for your life are within reach. Watch out for and don't fall into the traps, and without a doubt, you will reach your goal!

It's always the darkest before the dawn.

—Unknown

Weeping may endure for a night,
but joy comes in the morning.

—Psalm 30:5

Life's real failure is when you do
not realize how close you were to
success when you gave up.

—Unknown

Step 8

Don't Stop—Just Keep Swimming

Have you ever watched a superhero movie or any movie with a good and bad character in it? If you have, you probably have noticed that most American movies with this common story structure also have a few other things in common. One of those commonalities is that almost every hero/heroine reaches a moment during the movie when it seems as though all is lost. The character always seems to reach a moment when it appears as though they had wasted their time and that they should give up or turn back. This stands true in the famous 1976 movie ***Rocky***, starring Sylvester Stallone as the main character. He was an average Joe who wanted to use boxing to get a shot at elevating himself from his humble beginnings. During the main event, the fight that would make him a legend, he took quite a beating, and he suffered a detached retina and multiple injuries. He had many moments in which he could have quit. He could have decided that the beating he was taking was not worth it since his opponent would not go down, but this did not happen. This was not how Rocky wanted his story to end.

This same type of turn-back moment happened to King T'Challa, played by Chadwick Boseman, in the Blockbuster movie ***The Black Panther***. As a superhero movie, ***The Black Panther*** was not short on epic battle scenes. During one vitally important battle in the movie,

King T'Challa appeared to pay the ultimate price. It appeared that T'Challa's main rival (Kilmonger) defeated him. However, just like Rocky, neither King T'Challa, nor the multiple heroine characters in the movie, were willing to give up! Even in their darkest hour, they refused to let that one battle be the end of the story.

We could examine hundreds of movies—from ***Hidden Figures*** (2016) to ***Batman*** (1989) to ***The Avengers: End Game*** (2019)—this observation of a turn-back moment holds true. However, there are also another set of key things that American hero/heroine movies have in common. If you think about hero/heroine movies, you'll notice that this turn-back moment almost always happens in the latter half of the movie. The hero/heroine usually has had a few battles and a few wins before they are faced with THE THING or villain that can make or break them. It also at times appears as if that villain or whatever the hero has to battle has them licked. Basically, they get their behind kicked! Things are not exactly easy for them at this moment. During the turn-back moment, emotions are high and the viewer often connects with the pain, anguish, and feelings of defeat felt by the main character. It is at that moment the hero/heroine is faced with a choice. They can give up and let the chips fall where they may, or they can keep trying. They can choose the mundane, or they can choose the extraordinary. They can choose to push through and JUST KEEP SWIMMING! If they do, maybe—just maybe—they still have a fighting chance to win! Maybe they can be the hero after all!

Well, we all know what happens next, don't we? What happens next is what legends are made of. The hero/heroine rises from the ashes of what seemed like failure and defeat. They push on, and eventually, they are able to defeat the villain or the thing that loomed before them, threatening to hold them back. The hero/heroine wins the battle just when they could have been counted down and out. Just when they were about to give up and it seemed as though all was lost, they found just a little bit more grit and determination to power them on to victory.

Right before the victory, the hero/heroine/protagonist in the story didn't seem to realize that they were one hour and thirty minutes into the two-hour movie. They didn't seem aware of just how close they are to the end or to their goal. There was no whistle or bell that signified to them that they were in the final round or the final lap. All they knew was that they were tired, beat up, bruised, rejected, and dejected. They had the choice to either keep going and have faith that it would work out in their favor or they could quit and let all their work up to that point count for nothing.

I'm sure that you are thinking that all this sounds great, but what in the world does any of this have to do with you? If you were the kid that sat in front and center in English class in school, then you may have already made the connection. You might have been able to see how the analogies above connect to you and the movie that YOU are starring in. However, most are not nerds like I am (wink, wink), so I'll make it plain for you. You are the hero/heroine in the new story that you are writing. You are the star of your own movie. It is entitled ***How [insert you name] Makes It to His/Her Destiny***. Close your eyes and imagine "random movie voice guy" narrating the coming attractions! Like most movie trailers, there will be some laughs, some drama, and some action; but most relevant to this chapter, there will also be a villain or things you will have to defeat in your turn-back moment. Unfortunately for you, there is one more important detail: YOU are the hero. No one is coming to save you. Unfortunately, all the parts for the ***Fantastic Four*** and the ***Avengers*** were already filled. You are not a part of a hero posse. No slew of additional superheroes is on their way to rescue you. **<u>YOU</u>** ARE THE HERO. And just like the movies that were described above, you are going to reach a turn-back moment or two or FIVE. What will you do during that moment? Will you give up? Will you throw in the towel? Will you let all your work up to that point be in vain? Nope! YOU WILL NOT GIVE UP! You will be like Kathryn Johnson in the movie ***Hidden Figures***. You won't get close to victory and give up. You will work, you will push through, you will fight on, and you will win!

How do I know that you will win? Because unlike 80 percent of the US population who purchase a book, you read past chapter 1. You are already the cream of the crop! And as an additional insurance policy, you are going to write yourself a short note. A sort of time capsule, if you will. Please follow the directions below:

1. Take out a piece of lined paper. Please handwrite the letter—it needs to be personal. You need to feel yourself write the words. Trust me; it will have more meaning later.
2. Title the letter "Just Beyond This Wave—Just Keep SWIMMING!"
3. What is your overall vision/goal: (Fill in the blanks)?
4. What steps will you make to help get you there?
5. What is your WHY? Why do you have this vision? Who will it help? How will you be of service to yourself, your family, and your community? Why is this vision important to you?
6. What will you be giving up if you never reach your goal? Who will you disappoint?
7. What would you tell yourself to encourage yourself to keep going? What do you say to others when they want to give up on themselves?
8. What have you read thus far in this book that you think will inspire you to keep going?
9. Insert other inspirational quotes, sayings, or memories that you know will help you to keep going.
10. Write this as the last line on your paper in large letters: "You did not come this far just to quit. Remember, the toughest moments are often what you run into right before your miracle!"

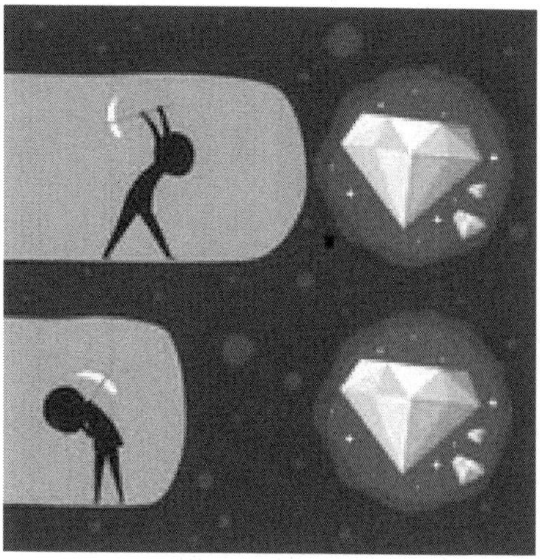

You never Know how close you are to
reaching your goal. Don't Give up!

Write this letter to yourself. Put a copy or two in a safe place. As you reach roadblocks, tough times, hurdles, and the dreaded turn-back moment, use this letter as your secret weapon. In the midnight hour when your emotions are high and you have no one to talk to, to vent to, or to encourage you. When you are drained and exhausted from trying to hold yourself up and keeping your dream in focus, when you reach a low point and can't find positive things to say about the challenge that is this journey, take out your secret weapon. Open the envelope and read this letter of encouragement about you, to YOU! Read it as many times as necessary to get it into your spirit. Read it until you feel the words of Beyoncé's song "Freedom" in your spirit, "Imma keep running, / 'cause a winner don't quit on themselves."

A Personal "Just Keep Swimming" Moment

In 2010, I had a two-year-old son and was somewhat freshly divorced. Yet I was determined to get a doctorate degree. Many folks thought I was nuts, but I had finally wrapped my head around the idea of it, and the thought of doing a dissertation no longer intimidated me. I had taken classes prior to starting the program, which gave me a pretty significant leg up, so much so that I only needed to take a few classes before I could start the most difficult part of the doctorate program, which was the actual dissertation. The dissertation was the final part of the process. It entailed conducting an action research project designed—run entirely by me. This meant that I would need to figure out a subject that I found interesting, pose an unanswered question about it, and design an experiment that would answer my hypothesis. I would then write an extremely detailed report, a five-chapter report, that would explain the whole process. As required, I selected a group of individuals to be on my dissertation committee and one as the chair of my committee that would help guide me through the process. This committee, for me, would be the gatekeepers to me being able to don the prefix ***Dr.***

As I was still somewhat young at the time (very early thirties), I had some laughable preconceived notions about how I thought the process would go. I was told by my committee members that, for most, it was a two-plus-year process. I remember being cocky and thinking I'll be done in a year, one and a half TOPS! Boy was I wrong! As I became entrenched in the process, which I referred to as Hazing 2.0 for me (wink, wink), I had many moments in which I was simply overwhelmed. I was a newly divorced, single mother. I was working a full-time job, conducting a research experiment during and after work hours, and spending an enormous amount of time writing and crunching data. But the worse part of it all, and why I called it Hazing 2.0, I would spend hours writing and researching to submit draft after draft to my committee to have it kicked back for additions and revisions over and over and over. I had so many revisions that I swore they asked me to put a sentence in my draft only to ask me to remove and then add it back in the next one to two submissions.

I had some interesting experiences while completing my doctorate. I had my entire beginning draft taken by a passenger by mistake while on a plane on my way to an intensive class. Talk about HYPERVENTILATING! But my worst moment came almost at the end of the process. I spent time, an enormous amount of time—as in having-relatives-watch-my-son-on-the weekend-so-I-could-write

TIME—working on these drafts. I had one member of my committee give me specific instructions on how to revise one of my chapters. I took detailed notes as usual so that I could follow the recommendations later. I spent about one to two months writing, revising, etc. At this point, this was my life. I had been working on my dissertation for nearly two years total. I was tired, worn out, frustrated by the process, and sick of looking at anything that had to do with my subject. I finally submitted the draft as requested, and the chair of the committee ripped it to shreds. She asked me why I had added some of the content that I did, said that I misunderstood her directions, and insisted that I needed to make major revisions—as in scrap 90-percent-of-what-I-had-just-spent-almost-two-months-on revisions! I wanted to take my phone, my computer, and everything related to my dissertation and drop it into the mouth of a volcano! The thing that made me the most frustrated was that I did exactly what she had asked me to do. I had the notes to prove it! It was the usual—add this, take this out, add this back. Why'd you add this? Oh yeah, well, that's OK. It was maddening, and it seemed like it would never end. However, I received one great piece of advice from another educator with her doctorate degree. She simply told me to JUST KEEP SWIMMING. When you want to quit, just keep swimming.

I was tired, I was frustrated, and it seemed like I was being hazed. After that last stunt, I didn't look at anything related to my dissertation for nearly three to four weeks, which was an eternity for me, since I had committed not to go more than two to three days without working on it for almost two years. I was having a turn-back moment. I was sick of it all! I was tired of not spending time with my son and my friends. I was tired of having no life because all my time was spent working on this dissertation. And for what? They were clearly toying with me at this point. They were making it difficult to get into their club, just because, and I was tired! But a little voice kept nagging me. "Just keep swimming," it said. "You have not come this far to quit," it said. Those voices grew louder until I had just enough strength to begin working again. And would you believe that after that turn-back moment, one month after my next submission, I was dubbed Dr. Ebony Potts? Just keep swimming!

Step 9

Personal Parables on a Vision Fulfilled

It is my sincere prayer that you have taken to heart the information that was contained in chapters 1 to 8 and will use it to help power you toward the vision and goals that you have for your life. There are plenty of concrete examples, parables, knowledge, data, ideas, and advice to help you along the way. However, the one piece that was missing, the one thing that can help drive things home (if you need one more push), is personal examples of how I was able to apply the lessons that I am sharing with you to achieve success in aspects of my own life. How did I climb my first few mountains? How did I start and move along my own path toward what I envisioned for myself? It is one thing for someone to regurgitate information that they have heard elsewhere, but it is a something completely different when someone speaks to you from experience. It is something else when someone can tell and explain to you how the information they are feeding you helped nourish them and others. As a parting gift, this is what I offer you. I hope that you can see a bit of yourself in my own mistakes and struggles, but I also hope that you can mirror my faith and perseverance. When all else failed, these are the things that helped me the most.

In each of the last few pages, I have selected moments in my life in which headings of some of the chapters were applied to my own situations and how they helped me to overcome. This by no means asserts that I am not still working on my own personal, most current vision for my own life. As you achieve and move toward your current vision, you'll be surprised at how that vision will morph and change shape. You will see that your vision is not a finite destination. You will continue to climb and to reach, just as I am. Once a goal-digger, always a goal-digger. Once you muster up enough strength to climb one mountain, you will undoubtedly set your sights on another taller one, and with each mountain conquered, your steps will become more sure, more rehearsed, and more clear. You will continue to grow, and your faith and patience will continue to be exercised and strengthened. As you become more sure of yourself, I hope you will reach back to help someone who may be stumbling, someone who is not quite so steady. This book is my hand extended to you and anyone else who may need assistance up their own personal mountain. Each story and example is to help steady you and reassure your steps. It is to let you know, you are not on your own. You've got this! Keep climbing!

My Vision

I have been envisioning and designing my life since I was a small child. I have been practicing the laws of attraction since I was in elementary school and didn't know it. I grew up with a grandmother who I'm sure was one of the Lord's angels. She was one of the sweetest, kindest women that I have met in my entire life, and she loved the Lord and the church immensely. Everyone in the small North Carolina town of Fairmont, knew Mrs. Rommie Hill. When I was eight years old, I spent a few weeks with my grandmother in the summer. In those few weeks, my grandmother introduced me to Christianity and faith in a way that only a grandmother could. By the time I went back home to my mother, I was baptized and knew what would become my favorite Bible verse: Philippians 4:13, "I can do all things through Christ who strengthens me." My grandmother taught it to me, and when she told it to me and I heard it in church, I absolutely believed it! As I child, I would sit in my room and imagine what my life would be like. I pictured different aspects of my life, and once I was done picturing them, I'd talk about them with those around me. My mom, dad, grandparents, godparents—whoever. Lucky for me, as a child, I never had anyone tell me that what I discussed wasn't possible. I never had anyone discourage me when I spoke of what my life would be like as an adult. I didn't have anyone to discourage me from speaking my life into existence. I was surrounded by such positive affirmations that the first time someone actually told me that I couldn't achieve something, I was a junior in high school and nearly a legal adult. It was then that a counselor informed me that I'd only get into one of the schools that I applied to on a wing and a prayer. I made it my business to prove her wrong, and I did! I not only got into the school she was referring to, I received my bachelor's degree from the College of New Jersey (formerly Trenton State University). I went on to end up married to a man that I envisioned and even produced the family I envisioned as a little girl playing in my room. I pictured myself happily married with one girl and one boy, and that is exactly what I ended up with. I envisioned every career move that I have ever made as well, every position that I have wanted wholehearted thus far, I have had. While I am actively working on my most current updated vision for myself and my family, I say all this to help you understand the power of the vision. Having a vision does not by any stretch of the imagination mean that everything will be smooth sailing. I certainly still had—and will continue to have—my own personal challenges that I will have to work through on this journey. But I can honestly say that there is nothing I have wholeheartedly wanted deeply that I envisioned for myself and/or my family for an extended time frame that I have not, at some point, held in my hand. I wanted a bachelor's, master's, and doctorate degree; and I was able to obtain them. I wanted a loving husband and two children; I was blessed with them. I wanted to become a school principal; I became one. I wanted to write a book, start a foundation—I could go on and on. The point is, don't doubt the power of suggestion. Don't discount the power of painting your own vision. Your life is a blank slate. Your life is a book with blank pages. You get to determine what is written. Before it is written in reality, practice your rough draft in your mind's eye. You'll be surprised at how your actual life will align with what you envisioned.

Faith

There are so many instances in which I have had to exercise faith in my life. So many that it was hard to pick just one example to include in this book. However, I was able to narrow down my instances to one of the most pivotal moments in my life. A moment that resulted in one of the biggest blessings that I have ever received.

This story began in the year 2013. I had just lost my mother suddenly and unexpectedly, so it was a very hard year for me. I was doing the best I knew how to pull myself out of a depression I had sunk into after my mother's passing. I had the support of many, including my father, godsister, best friend, and my fiancé, who became my husband that same year. Later that year, I was blessed to become pregnant with our first biological child together. I had an older son from a previous marriage and had a very pleasant physical pregnancy with him. I expected things to go just as smoothly with my second bundle of joy, but nothing was farther from the truth.

I had envisioned this little girl before I knew officially that she was a girl. I saw myself playing with her in the park with her Afro-puffs on a sunny day. The Lord had allowed me to see her before she had come to be. I saw her for the first time in my mind's eye when I was in elementary school. I knew in my heart from a young age that I was to have two children. However, on one of our early doctor's visits, the doctor we ended up later dubbing as Negatron, had declared that something was wrong. After subsequent visits and many tests, we were hit with what felt like a barrage of bad news. Our developing baby was undersized. She had an umbilical cord that only had two vessels in it instead of the standard three, which was "sure to continue to impede her growth" and could cause other complications. Upon examination of the fluid in my amniotic sac, it was determined that the baby also seemed to be mosaic (meaning present in some cells, not all) for a genetic disorder, Trisomy 16. Full-blown Trisomy 16 is one of the leading causes for miscarriage in women. They could not find that it was present in all her cells, but they could not tell what percentage of her cells were effected and what this would mean for her. It would, at the very least, most likely lead to preeclampsia for me and my baby. Preeclampsia is a condition in which the mother has a sudden increase in blood pressure, accumulates a build-up of proteins in her urine, and swelling in her hands and feet. If left untreated, it can lead to permanent organ damage and/or death of the mother and/or baby. This meant the increased likelihood of an early birth for a child that was already undersized and not developing at the usual rate. Last but not least, it was discovered that the baby had a large hole in the center of her heart that was effecting all four ventricles. "If she were to make it," as the doctor put it, she would very shortly after birth have to have surgery to repair the hole in order for her to live a normal life.

As you could imagine, this was not how I pictured my second pregnancy. With each additional visit, the doctor would be sure to remind us that she was growing, but not at a normal rate. He continued to remind me of the symptoms of preeclamsia. He also made me go to additional visits to monitor her movement to see if she was moving at a normal rate. Last but not least, he sat my husband and me down to have a serious conversation with us about the likelihood of carrying her full term. He paused while speaking with us about our "options," should we chose to exercise them.

We prayed, and we prayed hard! I knew what the Lord had showed me. Through it all, we focused on the vision that the Lord had provided us. When all else failed, and we were barraged with information that seemed to counter what we felt in our hearts, we didn't give in to the negativity. We focused on our faith. We never entertained the idea that our baby would do anything but grow to be the vibrant little girl that our faith told us she we would become. We could have easily sank into the negative news and reports, but we let it roll off of us like water off a duck's back. We focused on our faith, and I spoke positively to my baby and encouraged her to show that doctor who she was to prove them all wrong! This was one of the biggest exercises of faith that I have ever experienced. As a result of our investment and our belief, we have a beautiful, precocious, smart little girl, whom we have affectionately nicknamed Grown Lady Baby. Stay rooted in faith. Something beautiful and well worth it will be the result!

Fear

I guess you could say that I was always sort of a nerd. I was never the completely awkward type. I wasn't the get-shoved-in-a-locker, walk-out-the-bathroom-with-toilet-paper-stuck-to-my-shoes type of nerd, but I always loved school. According to my mother, I was like my dad, always wanting to know stuff, and I guess she was right. I enjoyed learning and loved every class (except for math—bleh!). My favorite time frame while I was in school was my junior and senior year in high school. I had the absolute BEST TIME! At that point, I was old enough to have figured out who I was, as much as possible at sixteen or seventeen years old, and had found my tribe. My friends and I spent all our time together, singing in chorus, joking around in the hall, running track, hanging out, and just blossoming into the young adults we were becoming. I loved it! I had obtained my license and had a newfound sense of freedom and responsibility. I was hypnotized by the buzz that we all felt, while planning senior activities, getting ready for the prom, getting a class ring, etc. The excitement about planning for our future was contagious. We were constantly filling out college applications, talking about who got into what college, and waiting for the annual senior paper that would list the plans of every senior in our school. I was excited, I was happy, and I was comfortable. I had become so comfortable that even though we talked daily about our future and what our plans were, I never actually took the time to realize that I would soon be thrusted into a world of unknowns. I knew that college would be a whole new and different existence, but for some reason, the gravity of what we were all about to face had not really registered.

After the annual chorale trip, the prom, and all the senior activities were done, THE DAY we had all been waiting for had come. Our high school graduation was upon us. I found myself standing in a hallway wearing my cap and gown. Standing near my friends laughing and joking, until I wasn't. At that instant, it finally registered what was about it happen. The day that we all said we couldn't wait for was about to happen, but then what? I had been in school with and known some of these people for over a decade, which, when you are eighteen, is more than half of your life. After this day, some of us would never see one another again. All the fun we had was about to end. We were about to be pushed out of the one thing that we all had in common—our high school—into a magnitude of unfamiliar people, places, and situations. At that moment, it all registered for me. I stood in the hallway waiting for the processional, trying to save face as the sadness of the end of high school and the fear of what was to happen next caused tears to well up in my eyes.

As we continued to stand and wait to file onto the football field, additional thoughts began to come to my mind. I told myself that heading out into the unknown was something that I had no choice but to do. My whole life was waiting on the other side of the unknown. I knew that I was not the only person graduating and heading into what seemed like the abyss. Many had graduated before me, and many will after me. I knew that even though what I was about to face was new, just like all things, the new eventually become the old. I knew in that moment that I would be OK.

As you embark on your journey, you will face your own individual graduation-day fears. You will be trying a new thing, going to a new place, and stepping out into a new journey, just like I did on the day of my high school graduation. But just like I reasoned with myself on that day about what I had to do, and why I had to do it, you will do the same. Your whole life is on the other side of the thing or the things that you fear. They can be overcome and conquered, and when you do, you will graduate to the next level in your life, placing you one level closer to the life that you envision for yourself. Don't let fear stop you!

Negative Self-Talk

In 2008, a gospel artist by the name of Donald Lawrence released a song called "Encourage Yourself." The opening words of the song are as follows: "Sometimes you'll have to encourage yourself. / Sometime you'll have to speak victory during the test. / No matter how you feel, / speak a word over your life and you will be healed. / Speak over yourself, encourage yourself in the Lord." This song is one of my favorite songs and pairs perfectly with this portion of the chapter. As discussed in chapter 7, we all have times in which no one is around, when we are left alone with our own thoughts. There is not a grown person that I have ever encountered that has not at had a down moment—a moment in which, negativity, anxiety, and a feeling of failure has not threatened to make you want to quit. We've all been there, most of us multiple times. I certainly have not been exempt from this fact. I've had to talk myself out of the hole more times than I can count. One particular moment that I remember occurred during my freshman year of college.

As I've already stated, I was kind of a nerd in grammar and high school. Things came kind of easy to me; however, I did not get straight *A*s. Not because I couldn't, but because I didn't really have anyone pushing me to do so. No one really stayed on me and explained to me about student loans, AP classes, etc., so I kind of coasted. I was only motivated to try really hard in my more difficult classes, which were physics and math. I received *A*s and *B*s pretty effortlessly. I never pulled all-nighters or had to study really, REALLY hard. When I arrived at the College of New Jersey, all that changed. I wasn't THE smart kid in the room. I was surrounded by THE SMART KIDS. My college was full of them. I was suddenly forced to try harder than I was used to. Trying to juggle being a first-generation college student meant working long hours, often without a lot of support, studying A LOT, and feeling overwhelmed. I remember calling my mom, informing her that they were trying to kill me in a half-joking manner. I was exhausted and stretched in ways I had never experienced before, away from everyone I knew, trying to make it through my freshman year as a biology major. At my weakest moment, when I was the most tired, frustrated, and exhausted, in came the negative thoughts. "You'll never graduate," "Your guidance counselor was right, you don't belong here," "You're going to flunk out like some of the other freshman." I called my mom many a day to vent and cry. However, one day, I got to thinking about all the knuckleheads from my high school that had made their way to and through college. The ones who sat in the back of the class and goofed off, etc., and I said to myself, "Are they smarter than me? How is it that they found a way to make it through and I was thinking about quitting?" I thought to myself, ***If they can do it, SO CAN I!*** I began to encourage myself. When I felt weak, I told myself that God didn't love me any less than those that came before me. If I wanted this degree, he would help me navigate and get it. This sentiment is one that I carried with me way beyond that time frame. It was and is true for me and is true for you also. It has become a sort of mantra for me, but you are welcome to borrow it (wink, wink). Anything that God is willing to provide for someone else or help someone else achieve, I can do and have the same. My path may not look the same, but if I can see it in my mind, I can hold it in my hand, so can you. When the sky gets dark and the clouds roll in, find a mantra, a saying to cling to, to help get you through. Don't let negative self-talk seep in and take over. Speak of your victory in the midst of the battle. Encourage yourself!

Step 10

Coming to Fruition

The sounds of trumpets blare, cue the lights, the dancers, confetti, and the fanfare! By the time you reach this page, you've reached your goal! The vision that you visualized in chapter 3 has come to pass! You did it! Your life has reached its pinnacle, and we got you there in a few days and just under ten chapters!

(Insert sarcastic smirk) If only it were just that simple. This sounds nice; in fact, it sounds GREAT, but I doubt that it's accurate. If I could lead folks to their wildest of wild dreams in the few days that it takes to read a 10 chapter book, I'd be well on my way to becoming the next Rockefeller, Warren Buffet, Oprah, or Bill Gates, or Mansa Musa (wink, wink)! However, by the time you reach the end of this book, you should have a clear picture of what it is you want and a very informed and well-thought-out idea of how to get there. Chapters 1 to 8 have led you on a very clear path and gave you steps to follow as you embark on the journey that leads to your specific vision for your life.

Chapter 1 helped to reiterate that the status quo you had been living previously was not, and is not, enough for you. Upon this realization, chapter 2 asked you to think about and/or discover your own unique talents and gifts. Once you focused your thoughts on your gifts and talents, you were asked to paint a picture in your mind's eye of the life of your dreams. What kind of life would make you the happiest and lift you the highest? Once you had a clear picture of how you would design your life to be if given the opportunity, chapter 4 challenged you to put faith into action and believe that what you saw in your mind's eye was possible. Once you were asked to truly believe in yourself and your ability to bring your vision to life, chapter 5 asked you to start mapping out a plan on how to make that dream a reality.

Chapters 7 to 8 were designed to help you take a peek into the future and anticipate some of the bumps that may come your way. Those bumps may come by way of people, situations, or your own fear of the unknown; but chapter 8 beckons you to just keep swimming. Last but not least, 9 gives concrete examples from my life in which I've had to apply the same principles you have read about to overcome obstacles in my own life to reach my goals and aspirations.

At this point, you are well prepared for whatever may come your way on your path to the mountaintop! When people set off on a path toward a goal, they often see their goal or vision as a final destination. They see it as a pinnacle, the top of the mountain. They often believe that once they get there, they will be set, all will be well, they will be happy, and everything will fall into place. While it is true that once you start to reach goals you have set for yourself and you start to see your vision come to pass, you will feel an enormous sense of pride, and rightfully so! When you work hard for something and you finally are able to see it, hold it, touch it, and live it, it is an indescribable feeling. And while this book can be seen as a very valuable tool as you work toward your vision, please know that the path to success is not a straight line. This is not meant to, nor should it, discourage you! But it is valuable knowledge that, once again, will help you to stomach, expect, and overcome the would-be barriers that will try to get in your way.

What does all this mean? Well, if you go to Google and type in the "path to success" and hit images, you will notice something. You will see that every image that comes up as a visual representation will be curvy. It will have road blocks and detours. You will also see statements about how individuals often believe that success is a straight shot. People think success is sort of like taking this book, reading it, and walking down the street where your dreams will be waiting for you, where you and success will hold hands and skip off into Forever-Ever Land. You and I both know that this is not the case. It wasn't the case before you read this book, and it won't be the case after you finish it. Those who are successful know that the path is curvy and that there will be barriers that will need to be conquered. Most who reach the finish line do so with battle scars, lessons, and knowledge they acquired along the way, which proves that they belong there. Successful individuals also know that the process to obtaining their success is also a cyclical one. Once you start to develop action steps, as you are asked to do in chapter 5, and this becomes a part of your path, please note that this process needs to be one of refinement.

If you set out to meet with a possible mentor and your approach does not work for the first candidate, the second, or the third, you would be a fool to approach the fourth person in the same manner, wouldn't you? If you try to grab a pie pan off the stovetop that you did not realize was still hot and you burn your hand, next time, you'll grab it with a potholder, won't you? If you still burn yourself with the potholder, won't you use a thicker one on the third try? You might even just decide to wait ten minutes before you try again. The point is, if your goal is goal/vision X and you design steps that you believe will lead you to goal/vision X, if after multiple spirited attempts you fail, you won't repeat those exact steps infinitely, hoping that things will someday change. Instead, you would review the steps, look for faults, make adjustments, and then try out the new steps you designed. If those steps work a little better but still don't quite reach your goal, you'll repeat this process, and you will cycle back. You will (1) design a process, (2) try it out, and (3) evaluate/assess how the process went; and if it doesn't work or help you reach your desired goal, you'll refine your process and go back to step 2. You'll try it again with your refinements. You will keep repeating this cycle until you reach your goal! I know all of that probably took you back to what some of you probably refer to as your boring science class where your teacher talked to you about the scientific method. As boring as it may sound, it is based on time and tested judgment, and it is a process that has helped humans discover and solve problems for hundreds of years.

The case of "How to make your vision a reality" won't be any different, Sherlock! (Wink, wink.) This cyclical method of problem solving by designing steps, trying out a process, evaluating/reassessing, drawing conclusions, and sometimes reevaluating has worked for hundreds of years; and it's something that anyone trying to achieve anything (with even a little bit J) of common sense does without thinking. Reading this, you are probably thinking, ***DUH!*** Of course that makes perfect sense; however, when people get into the woods of trying to make something work, solving a problem, or reaching for a goal, they at times forget this bit of information and try to rush through and over this part of the process. You, however, will remember this chapter and all the ones before it. You will remember all that you have learned in this book and use it to your advantage.

As you take all the nuggets of wisdom acquired from this book and those you pick up along the way independent of this book, remember that the vision you have for your life is a worthy and beautiful goal to reach for. It is nothing short of wonderful that you took the time and the effort required to get this far along your journey. However, as you start to reach milestones along your path, don't forget to recognize them, acknowledge them, and celebrate them. Don't wait until you reach the pinnacle or the mountaintop to stop and smell the roses and celebrate just how far you have come. You may not be at the top, but take time to celebrate the fact that you are no longer at the base of the mountain. You are NOT where you started, even just nine chapters ago! And on that glorious day when you finally reach the mountaintop, as I know you will, know that this is just the beginning! As you begin to realize your initial vision, that vision will morph and change shape. As this occurs, a new vision will begin to take shape. A whole new set of goals and design for your life will start to take shape. The process will not end there. It will only be the beginning. You will want more and/or something different, just like with anything else in life. Once you learned how to walk, not long after, you figured out how to run, jump, and climb. Once a mountain climber survives the climb to the top of Mount McKinley, the thought of climbing Mount Everest doesn't seem so ridiculous. Once a goal-digger reaches one goal, it is very unlikely that they will put down their shovel! As you achieve more, your dreams and imagination for what you can have, who you can be, and how you can evolve will stretch and grow also. You may think now, as you engage on this journey, that your goal is finite and that it has an end; but really, it will just be the beginning of a realization that the journey, the beautiful journey, really is as much a part of your vision as the goals you set for yourself. Take time to live, breathe, recognize, and celebrate life and your climb as you ascend to the highest and most fulfilled version of yourself. I pray blessings, enlightenment, and success upon you. I pray the same to all that use this text as inspiration to go after the life God promised to all who are willing to fertilize and birth the vision that he has placed inside of you!